ACCLAIM

for Rubenstein's

AGAMEMNON

"lively . . . vigorous . . . great directness. . . accessible to modern audiences"
—P. E. Easterling, Regius Professor of Greek, University of Cambridge, England

"vivid and immediate"
—Oliver Taplin, Professor of Classical Languages and Literature, University of Oxford, England

"brilliant!"
—Barry Bosworth, Director   Hills Acting Workshop, and teacher of The ⬛   ʼtion, Granite Hills High School, Califor⬛

A videotape oᶠ ⬛ Workshop performance of ⬛ ᴏf *AGAMEM-NON* is in the ⬛ ⬛es of Greek and Roman Drama, U⬛ ⬛, England.

THE ᴛᴙOJAN WOMEN

"Howard Rubenstein. . . not only conveys the story eloquently, but also nicely introduces the audience to the classic story and characters."
—Rob Hopper, *San Diego Playbill, Theatre News*

"I cannot speak too highly of Howard Rubenstein's simple, straightforward, and powerful English translation of Euripides' *The Trojan Women*."
—Eugene G. Schwartz, *ForeWord*

AGAMEMNON

ABOUT THE TRANSLATOR

Howard Rubenstein was born in 1931 in Chicago, where he attended Lake View High School. He was a *magna cum laude* graduate of Carleton College, where he was elected to Phi Beta Kappa and Sigma Xi and won the Noyes Prize for excellence in Greek studies. Rubenstein received his M.D. degree from the Harvard Medical School and has been a physician for over forty years, most of them at Harvard University. For several years he was a medical consultant for the State of California. He has published many articles and is the author of several books. Now retired from the practice of medicine, he lives with his wife, Judy, in rural San Diego County, California, where he writes and gardens. The Rubensteins have four grown children.

AGAMEMNON

A Play by AESCHYLUS
with Reconstructed Stage Directions

Translated from the Greek into English
with Introduction, Notes, and Synopsis

by
HOWARD RUBENSTEIN

Second Edition

Granite Hills Press™

AGAMEMNON
A Play by AESCHYLUS
with Reconstructed Stage Directions
Translated from the Greek into English
with Introduction, Notes, and Synopsis
by Howard Rubenstein

Published by Granite Hills Press™
P.O. Box P, El Cajon, CA 92022
Tel: (619) 442-0056; Fax: (619) 442-2392
e-mail: ghp@granitehillspress.com   SAN 298-072X
First Edition 1998 ISBN 0-9638886-4-1 LCCN: 96-95453
Second Edition 2003, ISBN 1-929468-07-5
Library of Congress Control Number: 2003091861
Cover by Brian Hiltz:
    front cover based on the First Edition front cover by Mary Brandes

Publisher's Cataloging-in-Publication Data

    Aeschylus.
      [Agamemnon. English]
      Agamemnon : a play / by Aeschylus ; with
    reconstructed stage directions / translated from the
    Greek into English with introduction, notes, and
    synopsis by Howard Rubenstein. -- 2nd ed.
      p. cm.
      Includes bibliographical references.
      LCCN 2003091861
      ISBN 1-929468-07-5

      1. Agamemnon (Greek mythology)--Drama.
    I. Rubenstein, Howard S., 1931- II. Title.

    PA3827.A8R83 2003   882'.01

Printed in the United States of America

To Judy

CONTENTS

ACKNOWLEDGMENTS

I am indebted to many people in translating *AGAMEMNON*. Countless scholars, known and unknown, made my work possible. I based my translation on the Greek text contained in the Loeb Classical Library, *Aeschylus II*. The English translations that were most useful to me were those by H. W. Smyth, Richmond Lattimore, and Edith Hamilton.

I am particularly indebted to H. D. F. Kitto, who began to review an early version of the manuscript in 1963, when he was a visiting professor of Greek drama at Brandeis University, Waltham, Massachusetts, and who completed the review in 1964, after he had returned to Bristol, England. Professor Kitto made many valuable corrections and suggestions that resulted in a greatly improved and more faithful translation.

I set the manuscript aside in 1965 because of my increasing responsibilities as a physician. Almost forgotten by me, it lay dormant until 1995, when my wife, Judy, discovered it. It was quickly awakened and underwent many subsequent revisions.

Since 1995, I am indebted to many people for identifying problems in my translation. These clear-thinking critics with no knowledge of Greek repeatedly drove me back to the Greek, usually to discover that Aeschylus was clear where I was not. The new revisions further improved the translation.

For the second edition, I have occasionally retranslated a word, phrase, or even a line, where further thought and consultation with the Greek text showed that other word choices were both more faithful and more clear. These changes are few and affect less than five percent of the first edition text. Also, I have revised some of the notes and added new ones where further explanation was needed. The Introduction has also been revised for the purposes of clarification and development of ideas.

While I cannot thank all the people who helped me — many people suggested a change in only one word, no mean contribution — I thank the following for editing one or more drafts: my daughter Jennifer Rubenstein, Mary Brandes, and Rebecca Rauff. Their questions and suggestions aided me greatly. I also thank my daughter Emily Rubenstein for computerizing the pedigrees of the major characters.

I especially thank Barry Bosworth, director of the Granite Hills Acting Workshop, for his appreciation of Aeschylus, for his faith in an unknown translator, and for staging the premiere of this translation in February and March 1997 in El Cajon, California. His creative and intelligent direction made me aware of the importance of stage directions for *AGAMEMNON*, and his directions formed the basis for many in this translation in both the first and second editions. Bosworth also identified the need for a prologue and epilogue for a contemporary audience and helped in writing them. Finally, during rehearsals, questions from Bosworth and the actors regarding the meanings of individual words or phrases resulted in revisions that gave the translation greater clarity.

I am also thankful to Robert Homer-Drummond, who directed the East Coast premiere at Palm Beach Atlantic University, West Palm Beach, Florida, in November 2002. Homer-Drummond made some suggestions and changes in directions that have been incorporated in the second edition.

Above all, I thank my wife, Judy, who edited all drafts of both editions and whose enthusiasm, questions, and suggestions helped solve many puzzles. Without her help, understanding, persistence, and patience, this translation would not have been completed, produced, or published.

Although I cannot adequately thank all the people who helped me in writing this book, I take sole responsibility for any errors it may contain.

INTRODUCTION

AGAMEMNON, written in classical Greek in the fifth century B.C., is the masterpiece of Aeschylus, who was the first writer of the form of literature that the Western world recognizes as plays. As such, he was the first playwright and the father of Western drama.

Aeschylus wrote plays in a living language that ordinary Athenians of his day could understand. His plays were popular in his time, and posterity exalts him. Hamilton writes, "No one else has struck such ringing music from life's dissonance" and "his insight into the riddle of the world has not yet been superseded" (*The Greek Way*, pp. 243 and 257). Kitto writes, "European drama knows no greater figure than Aeschylus" (*The Greeks*, p. 45). These are remarkable evaluations. And yet, at least in America, hardly anyone knows Aeschylus, and his plays are almost never performed. Why?

SOME CHALLENGES OF TRANSLATION

For most people, the existing translations are hard to understand, even the best of them. Translation is difficult, especially translating from classical Greek into English, and particularly translating Aeschylus. Puzzles abound. I have tried to solve them and to make a translation that is faithful to the original in meaning and, like the original, is written in a living language, as clear to ordinary people of today as the original was to Aeschylus' audiences.

The translator encounters many problems when translating classical Greek into modern English. Some of the most important are discussed on the following pages.

LEXICON

The classical Greek language died long before English was born. Modern Greek is more remote from classical Greek than modern English is from Elizabethan English (the language of Shakespeare), Middle English (the language of Chaucer), or Old English (the language of the author of *Beowulf*).

Therefore, a concurrent Greek-English dictionary was impossible, and none ever existed, a great handicap at the onset. Oxford scholars have done a heroic job in making a Greek-English lexicon with the help of intermediary languages, but there is no way to validate all of the word choices. Moreover, the problem is compounded because one word in Greek can stand for several words in English, and a lexicon, to be a versatile tool, needs to have them all.

The Oxford *Greek-English Lexicon* (Liddell and Scott) did not appear until as late as 1843. It contains the Greek words from ancient Greek writings and gives many of their equivalent words, often archaic, in English; for example, it contains the archaic English word for the foremost part of a ship's hull, *prow* — a word that makes contemporary American sailors uncomfortable — but it lacks the modern word for the same part of the ship, *bow*.

The *Greek-English Lexicon* has gone through nine editions, the latest in 1940; indispensable as it is, it remains incomplete. For example, not until after World War I, when the book was being considered for its ninth edition, did scholars recognize that the English vocabulary the *Lexicon* had used for Greek philosophy often did not correspond to the vocabulary that English-speaking philosophers themselves used, such as *determinism* or *free will*. In addition, much of the English vocabulary of farmers, archers, sailors, homemakers, and other workers still has not found its way into the *Lexicon*. Examples of English words not in the *Lexicon* that are important to Aeschylus' *AGAMEMNON* are *draperies* (see note 24) and nautical terms such as *to capsize* and *to run* (*before the wind*).   Readers wishing to explore this subject in greater depth should consult the "Preface 1925" by H. Stuart Jones in the *Greek-English Lexicon* (Liddell and Scott, 1940).

The only systematic way to make a more complete Greek-English lexicon would be to first make an English-Greek lexicon containing the important ordinary English words from all aspects of life that we share with the ancient Greeks.   Such a lexicon would reveal those English words missing from the Oxford *Greek-English Lexicon*, so they could be inserted into a subsequent edition of the *Lexicon*.   An English-Greek lexicon would also enable translators to easily find the classical Greek word for a modern English one.

Diction of Most Translations

Translations were usually written in neo-Elizabethan English until about the middle of the twentieth century. Perhaps translators thought archaic English words captured the antiquity of the Greek better than modern words did. Perhaps translators of Aeschylus thought archaic English words and neo-Elizabethan language were more majestic than ordinary English and therefore better captured Aeschylus' majestic Greek.   Whatever the reason, archaisms persist in the most modern of the translations.

Unfortunately, archaic English words in contemporary translations do not make the English lofty.   Instead, they debase the English by making it stilted and often unintelligible. They may also be unintentionally misleading, as the following example shows: As a high-school student, I was surprised to learn that the great Achilles, as described in English, had a *shaggy breast*, two words that translators of Homer obtained from Liddell and Scott's *Lexicon*. This phrase conjured up, in my adolescent and imaginative boy's mind, teats covered with wool, strange physical traits for a hero, and the very opposite of the image Homer is trying to convey.   British students and their teachers must have had similar difficulty with these words, because the abridged *Lexicon* (1958), which was designed for young students, contains the two modern and ordinary words needed to make the appropriate phrase in English — *hairy chest.*

In sum, the use of archaic words had the opposite effect from that which was intended, and ancient Greek literature was even further removed from the world of ordinary people and relegated to near oblivion on scholars' shelves. The irony is that classical Greek was a living language, no less so than modern English. To translate classical Greek literature faithfully, and in a manner that may make ordinary people want to read it, the translator must use the living words of a living language.

AESCHYLUS' METAPHORS AND DICTION

Aeschylus' metaphors can be breathtaking and often require a great deal of thought to be rendered into good English. I sometimes had to ponder the metaphors, and many of his straightforward ideas as well, for months, in some cases even years, in order to understand and express them well. In fact, in addition to Liddell and Scott's *Greek-English Lexicon*, thought and time were my greatest allies.

Aeschylus created metaphors from all aspects of life. He actively experienced life, observed it keenly, and loved, feared, and hated many things about it. He observed the heavens, the dawn, the night sky filled with stars, and he was filled with awe. He sailed the sea and experienced its beauty and treachery. He worked the soil and used the language of the farmer. He fought in battle and knew firsthand the toll of war on the battlefield and at home. He was religious in his own way and often spoke of Zeus as the Hebrew prophets spoke of God. He knew the complexity of the human heart and described accurately what it felt. He described anxiety and depression long before those emotional states were clinically identified; the chorus members' descriptions of their own moments of anxiety are remarkably clinical, and the portrait of Menelaus on his loss of Helen is an authentic portrait of an acute situational depression.

The great variety of emotions and ideas that Aeschylus describes are expressed with an economy of words characteristic of the classical Greek diction. Aeschylus' Greek, however lofty, is also lean and often condensed. Athenian audiences were accustomed to understanding the lean and condensed phrase, but the English-speaking audience is not. In order to make the Greek clear in English, each idea has to be teased out and set into separate English phrases or sentences.

AESCHYLUS' HUMOR

AGAMEMNON is filled with somberness and has moments of brooding, but Aeschylus is never lugubrious or sullen, and from time to time he will make us laugh. He punctuated his tragedies with humor, which must be recognized and expressed in translation (for example, see note 39).

IDIOMS OF CLASSICAL GREEK

We know little about Greek idioms. Some of the puzzles of translation exist because we have not yet deciphered certain idioms or have mistranslated them by being faithful to each word. Imagine the sentence "How do you do?" being translated into a foreign language by someone unfamiliar with English idioms.

On encountering a puzzle in the Greek, the translator may be tempted to translate the puzzle literally into English or not to translate it at all. The translator may justify this approach by attributing the difficulties to the word choices of Aeschylus or to corruptions in the manuscript. Unfortunately, these approaches do not solve the puzzle. Neither do they make a readable translation or a playable play.

In solving the puzzles of *AGAMEMNON*, I operated as if Aeschylus' words were always well chosen and the

Greek text were always intact. I carefully considered the context in which the puzzles existed and used that as a clue to their meaning, and I filled in the ellipses as meaningfully as I could. Thoughtful deliberation and sometimes discussion with other thoughtful people were the methods that worked best for me in solving the puzzles.

STAGE DIRECTIONS

Stage directions are essential to an understanding and enjoyment of *AGAMEMNON* even though Aeschylus' stage directions were lost long ago. Aeschylus probably designed choreography, composed music, and contributed to the set designs for his plays as well. These elements also have been lost.

Using the text as a guide and drawing on the ideas of Barry Bosworth, director of the Granite Hills Acting Workshop, and Robert Homer-Drummond, professor of theatre arts, Palm Beach Atlantic University, I have provided stage directions, suggestions for sets, and kernels of ideas for choreography. All are consistent with the text and have been dramatically effective during performances. They serve as a starting point for a director and should add clarity and pleasure for the reader.

PROLOGUE AND EPILOGUE

Finally, I have completely departed from Aeschylus in providing a prologue and an epilogue for *AGAMEMNON*. An Athenian audience of Aeschylus' day would have been familiar with the information these appendages contain, but a modern audience needs the context they offer. The prologue provides information necessary for an understanding of the play. The epilogue summarizes the main information that the final two plays of the *Orestea* provide and places *AGAMEMNON* in perspective in the trilogy.

THE LIFE OF AESCHYLUS (c. 525–455 B.C.)

PERSONAL

Very little is known about Aeschylus' personal life. He was born in Eleusis, a small town near Athens, where the Eleusinian mystery religions of Demeter and Dionysus were born. His father was named Euphorion and was a member of the nobility. We know nothing about his mother. Nothing is known about his wife or the quality of their marriage. Aeschylus' son Euphorion, who had the same name as Aeschylus' father, wrote tragedies, but none of his plays has survived.

WAR EXPERIENCE

During the Persian Wars, Aeschylus fought at the battle of Marathon in 490 B.C., and possibly later, in 480 B.C., at the battle of Salamis. There is no evidence that he participated in any other campaigns. Smyth comments wryly that when writers place Aeschylus at other battles, it is out of their need to romanticize and glorify him (*Aeschylus I*, p. xix).

RELIGIOUS PHILOSOPHY

Aeschylus' religious philosophy was well formed and original when compared with the mythological Greek religion of his day. The mythological cult religions known as the mysteries did not appeal to him; Aeschylus was devoted to the Olympian gods and to Zeus above all.

In a culture steeped in bird omens, prophecy, and sacrifice, Aeschylus tells us in *AGAMEMNON* that religion is more than the bird omens one interprets, more than the prophecies an oracle makes, and more than the animal or human sacrifices people make. He goes further. He decries prophecies and sacrifices. (For example, see notes 4–9, 11–13, and 15.) These were heretical ideas. Hamilton writes, "Aeschylus was profoundly religious and a radical, and so he pushed aside the outside trappings of religion to search into the thing itself" (*The Greek Way*,

p. 255).

Aristotle reports in *Ethics* that Aeschylus divulged in the theater some of the secret rites associated with the mystery religions. As a result, religious believers rose up against Aeschylus with the intent of killing him. Fortunately the case was transferred to the court of justice. Aeschylus' defense was that he had not known that the rites he spoke of were secret. This defense is not credible because everyone knew they were secret. Nonetheless, Aeschylus was exonerated, presumably because he had been a good soldier at the battle of Marathon and also because he was held in such high esteem as a playwright (see "Father of Drama," page 10).

DRAMATIC CAREER

Aeschylus' dramatic career began in 499 B.C. and continued for more than forty years. There is weighty evidence suggesting that his earliest extant play (and therefore the first extant play in Western literature) is the *Suppliant Maidens*, believed to have been produced around 490 B.C. Some scholars, citing newer evidence of dubious weight, believe his earliest extant play is the *Persians*, first produced in 472 B.C. (see "What Is the Oldest Extant Play?" page 15).

Aeschylus' last work, first produced in Athens in 458 B.C., two or three years before his death, is the trilogy the *Tale of Orestes* or the *Orestea*, of which *AGAMEMNON* is the first play. (This trilogy is more commonly spelled *Oresteia*, but I prefer the former spelling because it is equally correct yet simpler, just as *Medea*, the traditional way of spelling that play, is simpler than *Medeia*. Smyth, one of the great scholars of Aeschylus, also preferred *Orestea*.)

The total number of Aeschylus' plays was between seventy and ninety, of which seven are extant: the *Suppliant Maidens*, the *Persians*, *Prometheus Bound*, *Seven Against Thebes*, *AGAMEMNON*, the *Libation Bearers*, and *Eumenides*. The last three comprise the *Orestea*, the only extant trilogy from antiquity.

King Hiero the First, tyrant of Syracuse in Sicily, often invited famous poets to his court. Sicily was then a large Greek colony and part of Greater Greece. Around 475 B.C., Hiero invited Aeschylus to the city of Etna (now Catania) at the foot of Mt. Etna. For the occasion, Aeschylus wrote and produced his play *Women of Etna*. Aeschylus was invited a second time in 472 B.C., the year the *Persians* was first produced in Athens. Aeschylus went to Syracuse in 471 or 470 B.C. to supervise a production of the *Persians* in the theater in Syracuse (see photo, back cover), where ancient Greek plays are still performed.

LATER YEARS

In 458 B.C., shortly after the *Orestea* was produced in Athens, Aeschylus returned to Sicily, never to return to mainland Greece. He spent his remaining two or three years in the town of Gela. Why he retired to Sicily is unknown. Some have suggested that at this time in his life he saw his fame in Athens diminishing while that of his younger contemporary Sophocles was increasing, which rankled him. Perhaps he had offended the orthodox religious believers in Athens by the radical ideas expressed in the *Orestea*, especially in *AGAMEMNON*. In Sicily, he was accepted and welcomed; there his plays were performed to adulation, and he basked in fame. Perhaps he had become disenchanted with Athenian democracy, which he did not see as sufficiently democratic. Perhaps he enjoyed the beauty and lushness of Sicily as opposed to the barrenness of Athens.

DEATH

Aeschylus died and was buried in Gela in 456 or 455 B.C., at the age of about seventy. There is a legend that he died accidentally when an eagle, mistaking his bald head for a rock, dropped a tortoise upon his head to crack open its shell. This legend may have been invented

by those who wished to punish Aeschylus for his contempt for bird omens.

Aeschylus' epitaph said: "Beneath this memorial
stone lies Aeschylus, Euphorion's son, the Athenian, who
perished in the wheat-bearing land of Gela. The sacred
field of Marathon can speak of his valor in battle — and
so can the Persian with his thick head of hair." Some say
that the people of Gela wrote the epitaph, others that the
poet himself wrote it. Sidgwick ("Aeschylus," p. 272)
argues that it was written by Aeschylus because only a
poet would praise the soldier and keep silent about the
poet. In support of Sidgwick's judgment, I would add
that the epitaph's imagery is somewhat startling and in-
cludes a touch of humor, two characteristics of the writing
of Aeschylus.

After Aeschylus died, two great tributes were paid to
him:

First, immediately following his death, a decree was is-
sued in Athens announcing that Aeschylus' plays could
be revived and produced anew at the Athenian dramatic
festivals. Only Aeschylus was awarded this honor. Prior
to his death, only new plays could be produced at the festivals.

Second, in 425 B.C., thirty years after Aeschylus died,
Aristophanes wrote a comedy called the *Acharnians*. The
main character, an old man who happens to be a writer of
comedies, like Aristophanes, says that in his lifetime, although things as numerous as grains of sand on the beach
have annoyed him, only four things have delighted him.
One of these four is the plays of Aeschylus. Then, grum-
bling about his countless complaints, this character relates
how one night he went to the theater fully expecting to
see a tragedy by Aeschylus, but on taking his seat, discovered that the play he was about to see had been written by
someone else!

Aristophanes paid a further tribute to Aeschylus in his
play the *Frogs*, where he describes a fictional contest in
the underworld between Aeschylus, Sophocles, and Eu-

ripides to determine which of the three was the greatest
playwright. Aeschylus emerges victorious.

"FATHER OF DRAMA"

Theater in the West began with Greek drama — and
Greek drama began with tragedy. During the sixth and
fifth centuries B.C. (and perhaps earlier), tragedy evolved
from lyric poetry recitations that were part of the religious
rites devoted to Dionysus, the God of Wine, and the mystery religion surrounding him.

During these Dionysiac rites, lyrical verses, full of
bombast and "laughable diction" (to use Aristotle's
phrase in his essay *Poetics*, p. 43), were sung, at first probably by only one person, then by two, three, and more
until there were fifty singers. The verses or poems sung
by a group of fifty were called *dithyrambs*. (Dithyramb is
another word for Dionysus.) In time, in addition to
singing lyrical verses, the group of fifty began to dance in
a circular area, accompanied by musical instruments, particularly flutes. During these rites a goat, an animal special to Dionysus, was sacrificed to the god, and the
dancers wore goatskins to represent satyrs (half-goats
half-men), mythological beings that delighted Dionysus.

The traditional chorus of Greek tragedy evolved from
the recitation of the dithyrambic poems and from the
dithyrambic dancing. The choral odes evolved from the
dithyrambs or poems to the wine god. The word *chorus*
is derived from "dancers on a circular area," and the
word *tragedy* is derived from "goat-song."

Thespis, who lived in the sixth century B.C., was the
first writer to have a leader step forth from the body of
the chorus to deliver important lines that were in agreement with the odes of the chorus. Thespis then added a
single character in addition to the chorus leader. This
character, like the leader, had monologues that agreed
with the chorus. These monologues, like the important
verses of the chorus leader, augmented the theme and
provided emphasis in order to increase the dramatic inter-

est. However, his works contained no dramatic conflict.
Thespis' most famous student was Phrynichus, who made
no known innovations on his master.

Aristotle, who lived a century after Aeschylus, does
not mention Thespis or Phrynichus in his description of
the rise of tragedy. Aristotle had to have known about
them. The significance of Aristotle's omission is that he
thought them unworthy of consideration.

In *Poetics*, Aristotle teaches that tragedy came about
through evolution, moving from "laughable diction" to
"grandeur" (p. 43). Aeschylus is the first tragedian
Aristotle calls by name:

> Aeschylus innovated by raising the number of
> actors from one to two, reducing the choral com-
> ponent, and making speeches [and not choral
> odes] play the leading role (*Poetics*, p. 43).

Aristophanes, a contemporary of Aeschylus, says that
serious tragedy began with Aeschylus. In Aristophanes'
play the *Frogs*, the leader of the chorus says to a character
playing Aeschylus,

> O you who were the first of the Greeks to build
> majestic words into towers and create tragedy
> from a world of nonsense! [translation mine]
> (ll. 1004–5).

Murray, the twentieth-century Greek scholar, speaks
of Aeschylus as the "creator of tragedy":

> When Aeschylus is called the 'creator of tragedy,'
> it can hardly be meant that . . . he was the first
> writer of Greek tragedy. There were several mak-
> ers of tragedy before him, Phrynichus, Choirilus
> [sic], Pratinas, and, earlier than all, Thespis.
> The claim made for [Aeschylus] is a much

greater one: that in the artistic or imaginative sense, he created the form of literature that we now call tragic (*Aeschylus: The Creator of Tragedy*, p. 1).

Murray becomes more specific:

[Aeschylus] cared greatly about philosophic or religious truth, as well as about beauty, and used his art for expounding it. . . . Aeschylus [gave us the] gift of . . . majesty where it was not before (pp. 18–19).

Smyth, another twentieth-century scholar of Aeschylus, calls Aeschylus "the true founder of the drama" (*Aeschylus I*, p. xxvi). Smyth gives the following reasons:

The art as [Aeschylus] received it . . . consisted almost exclusively of choral songs varied with interludes of narrative, together with some brief dialogue between the leader of the chorus and a character impersonated by a single actor. . . . The art, as [Aeschylus] left it, had well-nigh attained to its fullest capacity (p. x).

His successors might work in the light of his achievements. . . . [But he] owed the direction of his craftsmanship to none greater than himself. He was, in a word, the legislator of . . . tragedy (p. xiv). . . . the true founder of the drama (p. xxvi).

Both his style and his content set Aeschylus above and beyond his predecessors, who were pioneers.

In *AGAMEMNON*, Aeschylus expresses ancient concerns that remain modern and relevant today. His questions include the following: What is the difference between vengeance and justice? How do the gods deal with people who commit murder? Is there divine retribution for the murder of an individual — or for the murder of a nation? What is the divine purpose of human suffering? How do people assume responsibility for their acts if predetermination reigns? Do the gods care about mankind? What is the source of evil? And, most modern of all, are women as powerful as men, or even more powerful? The evidence shows that none of Aeschylus' predecessors or contemporaries were interested in such great philosophical questions.

In addition to asking these questions, Aeschylus makes some philosophical observations, such as: Wealth is not the sin; greed is. Ambition and the bold deeds that come from it are not the sin; blind ambition and the reckless deeds that come from it are.

Aeschylus' philosophy is often highlighted through aphorisms in the speech of the chorus. His philosophical problems are ones that philosophers still wrestle with today. Curiously, philosophers do not acknowledge how great a philosopher Aeschylus was, perhaps because they feel that philosophy is the province of philosophers, not artists.

In spite of the reasons advanced by Aristotle and Aristophanes in antiquity, and Murray and Smyth in the twentieth century, some scholars have been reluctant to give Aeschylus the title of father of drama on the grounds that there were other dramatic writers contemporary with him, most notably Phrynichus, or even preceding him, including Choerilus, Pratinas, and most notably Thespis. These scholars summarily dismiss the ancient and modern evaluations even though these evaluations are supported by evidence. These scholars seem to attach more value to precedence than to significance, and they do not discriminate between a recitation and a play.

In sum, in my judgment Aeschylus deserves the title *father of drama* or *creator of tragedy* or *founder of the drama* because the evidence shows he revolutionized the theater in multiple ways: Aeschylus was the first to move beyond recitation, the singing of songs, and the dancing of dances. He was the first to integrate all these activities into a coherent play in which multiple actors participated in addition to the chorus. He was the first to have his characters engage in dialogue that showed conflict. He was the first to make tragedy beautiful, in large part by the majesty of his language. Finally, he was the first to make his plots especially meaningful by infusing them with religious philosophy.

WHAT IS THE OLDEST EXTANT PLAY?

The oldest extant play in Western civilization is by Aeschylus. But which play? That is the subject of a fascinating controversy.

Until the middle of the twentieth century, most scholars considered the *Suppliant Maidens* to be the oldest extant play, dating it to c. 490 B.C. This selection and dating were based on the following three reasons:

1. The chorus in the *Suppliant Maidens* contains fifty members. This large size is characteristic of the most primitive choruses, dating from the sixth century B.C.

2. The chorus in the *Suppliant Maidens* has the leading role and also has more than half the lines, two more characteristics of a primitive work.

3. Aristotle, in his *Poetics*, states that "Aeschylus innovated by . . . reducing the choral component" (p. 43). It is not clear whether Aristotle means a reduction in size (number of members) or in importance. Either way, a small chorus of twelve to fifteen members having a secondary role would be characteristic of a more modern play, whereas a chorus of fifty members having the leading role would be characteristic of a more primitive one.

By these criteria, the *Suppliant Maidens* would be among Aeschylus' older plays, while the *Persians*, *Prometheus Bound*, and the plays of the *Orestea*, each with a chorus of twelve to fifteen members that has a secondary role, would be among his later plays.

In 1952, a document was discovered that in the eyes of some scholars challenged the position of the *Suppliant Maidens* as the oldest extant Western play. The document is a papyrus fragment that has been identified as a *didascalia*, a list of winners in a dramatic contest in ancient Athens. The particular fragment under discussion records the results in an unknown year in which the winners were Aeschylus for first prize and Sophocles for second. The didascalia names Aeschylus' winning play or trilogy — it is not clear which — as *Daughters of Danaus*. The name *Suppliant Maidens* does not appear on the fragment, and neither does the name of the play by Sophocles.

Nonetheless, some scholars maintain that the didascalia proves that the *Suppliant Maidens*, in spite of its primitive qualities, should be dated at 468 B.C. or later. As a result, the *Persians*, another play by Aeschylus, dated at 472 B.C., has become known as the oldest extant play. Almost all drama and reference books today list the *Persians* as such. To ascertain whether this change is justified, we must examine the thinking of the advocates of the change — those who cite the didascalia fragment as evidence.

These scholars make two major assumptions. First, they assume that the *Daughters of Danaus* mentioned in the fragment is a trilogy containing the *Suppliant Maidens*. They also assume that the Sophocles named in the fragment is the famous Sophocles whose plays posterity knows and acclaims, even though there were other playwrights with the name Sophocles and the fragment does not include the title of Sophocles' play, which might help to identify which Sophocles he was.

Having made the above two assumptions, the advocates of the didascalia reason as follows: Because the famous Sophocles' first play was produced in 468 B.C. (an established fact), the didascalia fragment must pertain to a contest held in that year or later. Thus, the *Daughters of Danaus* (assumed to be a trilogy including as one of its plays the extant *Suppliant Maidens*) must have been produced in 468 B.C. or later. Since the *Persians* was first produced in 472 B.C. (an established fact), the *Persians* must be at least four years older than the *Suppliant Maidens*. Therefore, the *Persians* must be the oldest extant play.

Let us examine five reasons why this conclusion is not warranted:

1. As previously discussed, the size and role of the chorus in the *Suppliant Maidens* are characteristic of a more primitive play, while the size and role of the chorus in the *Persians* are more typical of Aeschylus' later plays.

2. The didascalia fragment's *Daughters of Danaus* may not have been a trilogy containing the *Suppliant Maidens*. It could have been a different trilogy or play with a similar theme.

3. A play was not necessarily produced in the same year it was written. Sophocles' *Oedipus at Colonus* was not produced until five years after the author's death. The *Suppliant Maidens*, similarly, could have been written early in Aeschylus' life and not produced until much later, even after his death. (Perhaps Aeschylus was dissatisfied with this play or viewed it as an exercise because of its primitive character and decided not to produce it, but after his death, because of his fame, his sons decided to produce it.)

4. Aeschylus' plays, unlike those of other playwrights, were permitted to be produced repeatedly after his death, even if they had premiered while he was alive. Therefore, even if a play by Aeschylus was produced and won a contest in the same year as a play by Sophocles, we cannot be sure if the production was a premiere or a revival.

5. The Greek playwrights sometimes wrote two versions of a play. For example, Euripides wrote two versions of *Hippolytus*, Sophocles wrote two versions of the *Oedipus* myth, Aristophanes wrote two versions of *Clouds*, and Aeschylus wrote two trilogies on the *Prometheus*

theme. Perhaps Aeschylus wrote two versions of the *Suppliant Maidens*, calling the second one the *Daughters of Danaus*. Perhaps the second version was performed at the contest noted in the didascalia, a version in which the chorus had been "diminished" and the characters and their dialogue had been increased — in short, a version considerably different from and more modern than the extant *Suppliant Maidens*. Posterity does not necessarily possess the most updated version of a playwright's plays.

In summary, in my judgment, the didascalia fragment provides no evidence regarding the first production date for the extant *Suppliant Maidens,* let alone the date when it was written. The fragment therefore does not prove that the extant *Persians* is more ancient than the extant *Suppliant Maidens*.

To read more deeply on this subject, see Garvie, who provides diagrams, descriptions, and interpretations of the didascalia fragment in *Aeschylus' Supplices: Play and Trilogy*. Garvie himself concedes, "The *Supplices* [*Suppliant Maidens*] may have been written early, but not performed till late in Aeschylus' life" (p. 25). He makes the same concession a second time: "we cannot definitely rule out the possibility that the *Supplices* was written early and produced late" (p. 26). Having made this concession, Garvie shows that the didascalia fragment proves nothing and provides no evidence that the *Persians* is the oldest extant play. Therefore, the *Suppliant Maidens*, still supported by the data and reasons that have always supported it, holds its distinctive position as the oldest extant play in Western civilization.

AGAMEMNON

The plot of *AGAMEMNON* is well crafted and simple. Greece has won the Trojan War. The news reaches Greece via a relay of beacons lit on mountaintops at intervals between Troy and Greece. Agamemnon, commander in chief of the Greek army, returns home a conquering hero. He brings with him a mistress, the Trojan princess Cassan-

dra. His wife, Clytemnestra, kills them both: Agamemnon because ten years earlier he killed their daughter
Iphigenia, and Cassandra because she is Agamemnon's
mistress. Aegisthus, Clytemnestra's lover and Agamemnon's cousin, reveals yet another reason why Agamemnon deserves to be murdered: Agamemnon's father
(Aegisthus' uncle) murdered Aegisthus' siblings and
served them as food to their father.

  AGAMEMNON spans probably several weeks from beginning to end. It lends itself to three acts because there
are two natural divisions in the play.

  The first division comes after the beacon fires announce the victory of the Greeks, but before the Greek
army arrives home from Troy. There is an interval of
several weeks, or however long it takes for an army to set-
tle down after victory, pack its gear, gather its slaves, store
fresh water and other provisions for the voyage home,
make ship assignments, embark from Troy, and sail home
to Greece — encountering numerous setbacks along the
way, including a terrible storm at sea. It takes Ulysses ten
years to sail home to Ithaca from Troy, but he faces extraordinary obstacles. Achilles estimates that with fair
weather and calm seas (and no unexpected problems), it
will take him three days to sail home to the port town of
Phthia (Homer, *Iliad*, Vol. I, Book IX, l. 363). Agamemnon has farther to sail. He has to sail to the port town of
Argos. So with favorable sailing conditions, the voyage
might take him about a week. But conditions are not favorable. A terrible storm strikes that almost annihilates
his fleet.

  The second division comes at the suspenseful moment
when Agamemnon enters the palace and the audience
asks the question, is vengeance going to triumph?

AGAMEMNON AND THE UNITIES

  Readers who are concerned with the traditional literary
doctrine of the unities may be surprised to discover that
AGAMEMNON violates the *unity of time*, which dictates

that a tragedy take place within a single day. The *Orestea* actually violates the unities of both time and place. The *unity of place* dictates that a tragedy take place in one location. The second play of the trilogy, the *Libation Bearers*, begins several years after *AGAMEMNON* ends; the third play, *Eumenides*, does not take place in Argos as *AGAMEMNON* and the *Libation Bearers* do, but in two different locations, Delphi and Athens.

Any so-called violation of the unities, however, is anachronistic. These rules were invented by the French Academy for French classical theater more than two thousand years after Aeschylus wrote his plays. French rules cannot be expected to apply to Aeschylus.

The French scholars claim to have based their rules on those in Aristotle's *Poetics*. Aristotle lived a century after Aeschylus and greatly admired him. It is curious that Aristotle would have written such rigid rules that would not apply to Aeschylus. Aristotle, in fact, does not define the unities as the French Academy ascribes them to him. Regarding the unity of time, Aristotle writes, "Tragedy tends so far as possible to stay within a single revolution of the sun, or close to it" (p. 47). *So far as possible* is an escape clause of such magnitude as to make the so-called unity of time meaningless. Regarding the unity of place, Aristotle says nothing.

Shakespeare, who lived more than twenty centuries after Aristotle and is considered by many to be the greatest playwright since Aeschylus, did not follow the unities. Insofar as the unities do not apply to two of Western civilization's greatest playwrights, the unities clearly are not essential to great drama.

SYNOPSIS

BACKGROUND

AGAMEMNON is the first of three plays in a trilogy about the family of King Atreus and the curse on the House of Atreus that spans three generations: Atreus (Agamemnon's father), Agamemnon, and Orestes (Agamemnon's son). The three plays are named the *Tale of Orestes* or the *Orestea* because it is Orestes who is instrumental in bringing the curse to an end.

AGAMEMNON takes place in Argos, Greece, around 1200 B.C., immediately after the Trojan War has ended. The Greek king Agamemnon, commander in chief of the Greek army, victorious at Troy, returns home a conquering hero. What reception awaits him?

Before *AGAMEMNON* begins, three major events have occurred that are alluded to throughout the play and have a major impact on the action of the play. These events are referred to in Greek mythology as *Thyestes' feast*, the *elopement of Helen and Paris*, and the *sacrifice of Iphigenia*.

THYESTES' FEAST

Atreus, king of Argos, father of Agamemnon and Menelaus, was challenged in his rule by his brother Thyestes, who also made love to Atreus' wife. Enraged at this treachery, Atreus banished Thyestes.

In time Thyestes returned to Argos with his little children, begging forgiveness. Atreus pretended to forgive him but instead prepared a horrible revenge. He prepared a feast of reconciliation, but the roast he served was the flesh of Thyestes' own children — Thyestes' feast. On discovering the gruesome nature of the food he was eating, Thyestes placed a curse upon the House of Atreus and returned into exile with his one surviving child, the infant Aegisthus, cousin of Agamemnon and Menelaus.

ELOPEMENT OF HELEN AND PARIS

Some years after Thyestes' feast and about ten years before the play *AGAMEMNON* begins, Agamemnon and Menelaus, sons and successors of King Atreus, were ruling together as joint kings of Argos.

To their palace came a guest, Paris, a young and handsome prince of Troy. Troy was a walled city, the wealthiest nation of the ancient Western world, located on the eastern shore of the Aegean Sea at the strategic entrance of the Dardanelles in what is now Turkey. Helen was the wife of Menelaus and the most beautiful woman in the world. Paris and Helen fell in love and eloped to Troy.

To avenge Paris' abuse of hospitality, Agamemnon raised a mighty Greek army to storm the walls of Troy, plunder its riches, recapture Helen for his brother Menelaus, and win glory for himself. The elopement of Helen and Paris precipitated the Trojan War, which lasted ten years.

SACRIFICE OF IPHIGENIA

Helen and Paris easily escaped from Greece because a boat was waiting to carry them to Troy, and they had a favorable wind. However, by the time the Greek army had assembled and was ready to sail to Troy, a violent storm had arisen, making sailing impossible.

Calchas, the prophet of the Greek army, advised Agamemnon to sacrifice his daughter Iphigenia to the goddess Artemis in order to calm the storm and obtain favorable winds. (Curiously, Calchas did not interpret the storm as an omen showing that Artemis opposed the Trojan War.) Agamemnon, although conflicted, ordered the sacrifice of Iphigenia. Iphigenia was slain on the altar.

The storm subsided and a fair wind ensued. Agamemnon and the Greek army sailed to Troy (see note 15).

Agamemnon's wife, Clytemnestra, perceived the death of Iphigenia not as a sacrifice to a goddess but as the wanton murder of their child. Many of the Greeks at home agreed with her.

During the ten-year war, Clytemnestra ruled cruelly and took a lover, none other than Aegisthus, Agamemnon's cousin and the sole surviving brother of the children who were eaten in Thyestes' feast. Clytemnestra and Aegisthus collaborated to bring vengeance upon Agamemnon: Aegisthus to avenge his siblings, and Clytemnestra to avenge her daughter Iphigenia. They conspired to murder Agamemnon.

ACT ONE

As the play begins, it is a starry night, just before dawn, in Argos, Greece, in front of the palace of King Agamemnon, ten years after the onset of the Trojan War.

The sentry complains of the long war and his ten-year vigil. He is watching a distant mountaintop for the appearance of a bonfire, the last in a prearranged series of bonfires on mountaintops from Troy to Greece that will relay the announcement of the victory of the Greeks. He hints that things have not been going well under Queen Clytemnestra's rule. Suddenly he sees a fire on the mountaintop. Realizing that this is the beacon for which he has been watching all these years, he pounds on the palace doors in great excitement to announce the news to the queen.

Clytemnestra's attendants light torches and lamps in the palace courtyard. The chorus, consisting of old people, is attracted to the palace by the torches.

While awaiting the queen's explanation of all the lights, the chorus recounts the elopement of Helen and Paris, the terrible war that ensued, and the sacrifice of Iphigenia. The chorus explains that such painful events are not without benefit to mankind because Zeus has established the law that "Wisdom comes through suffering" (p. 51).

The prophet of the chorus (who reveals himself as Calchas) explains why he proposed the awful sacrifice of Iphigenia. He reviews his interpretation of "the omen of the birds" (p. 47; notes 5–7 and 11): Two eagles ripped open a pregnant hare and feasted on her. The two eagles symbolized the two kings, Agamemnon and Menelaus. The killed hare symbolized Troy, wantonly destroyed by the two kings. Artemis sent a foul wind to prevent the Greeks from sailing to Troy. Calchas suggested that to appease Artemis and to gain a fair wind, Agamemnon should sacrifice his daughter Iphigenia.

The members of the chorus find Calchas' interpretation of the omen of the birds not sacred but evil. They call the sacrifice of Iphigenia "worse than the bitter storm" (p. 52) that prevented the Greeks from sailing to Troy. The chorus members repeatedly state that they hate the Trojan War — the "war waged for a woman" (p. 54) — with its unnecessary carnage for Greeks as well as Trojans, and they attribute the sacrifice of Iphigenia to Agamemnon's "unbridled ambition" (p. 53).

The narrator describes Agamemnon's conflict over the proposed sacrifice of Iphigenia, concluding that Agamemnon's "unbridled ambition" (p. 53) made the choice for him. Agamemnon rationalized murdering his daughter for the sake of his army: "Yet, how can I fail fleet and friends? They urge sacrifice of innocent blood, and that is just" (p. 53). Moreover, Agamemnon said that Fate demanded this sacrifice. The narrator continues the story: Iphigenia was sacrificed on the altar. The storm subsided. The winds shifted. The army sailed to Troy.

Clytemnestra appears and describes the course of the beacon fires (pp. 58–63) and explains their meaning: they announce that the war with Troy is over and the Greeks are victorious. The chorus members can hardly believe their ears. Then Clytemnestra becomes reflective and sympathizes with the terrible suffering of the Trojans. She prays that the Greeks behave well in victory, that they not despoil the Trojan temples, and, by implication, that they not rape the Trojan women. Knowing that the Greeks still have ahead the dangerous voyage home, Clytemnestra worries that the curses of the Trojan dead could yet vanquish the Greek victors.

The chorus decries the evil consequences of war: not only the dead on the battlefield but also the grief of their families at home.

Act One ends with the chorus predicting doom to those who cause doom and citing the "retribution of Zeus" (p. 67), who demands punishment for crimes.

ACT TWO

Act Two begins several weeks later. The chorus is assembled in the palace courtyard, doubting that Clytemnestra's beacons truly signaled the fall of Troy.

Suddenly a herald of the Greek army enters the city gates. He announces the victory of the Greeks at Troy, thereby confirming the beacon message, and he also announces the imminent appearance of Agamemnon and other survivors. The herald describes the suffering inflicted by the war in battles at Troy and also by the storm at sea on the voyage home, when many Greeks who had survived the war drowned. Others remain missing, including King Menelaus.

Clytemnestra scoffs at the herald for bringing news that she announced so clearly weeks earlier. She tells the herald to take a message to Agamemnon to come quickly "to your queen, as true today as the day you left" (p. 83). Everyone at home knows that Aegisthus is her lover, and the chorus is shocked at her blatant lies. The herald, believing the queen, departs to deliver her message.

The chorus recalls the elopement of Helen and Paris and the resulting unpopular war and unnecessary destruction of Troy. The chorus observes that "Evil comes from evil" (p. 92) and "Righteousness brings all things to their just conclusion" (p. 93).

Trumpets sound. Agamemnon makes a triumphal entrance in a chariot (p. 94). At his side is Cassandra, a young, strange, and beautiful princess of Troy, now Agamemnon's personal slave and mistress; she remains immobile throughout Act Two. Ironically, Cassandra is the sister of Paris, who came to the same palace more than ten years earlier as an honored guest. Cassandra is famous as the prophet who always prophesies the truth but whom no one ever believes. Also accompanying Agamemnon is a retinue of his soldiers, survivors with him on his ship. The leader of the chorus greets Agamemnon and reveals his early opposition to the war, but he now welcomes Agamemnon home for a job well done in conquering Troy.

Agamemnon expresses joy at being home and greets everyone in the courtyard except, noticeably, Clytemnestra. He thanks the gods for victory, describes the conquest of Troy by means of the great wooden horse, and expounds on the importance of loyal friends.

Clytemnestra boldly tells a series of lies: how she suffered in Agamemnon's absence, how faithful she has been to him, and how she had to send away their only son, Orestes, to protect him from possible rebellion at home (when it is obvious she only wished to protect him from witnessing her adultery). She makes a great display of love for her Agamemnon, first in words, then by groveling in the dust before him, a behavior uncharacteristic of Greeks.

Clytemnestra has her attendants lay beautiful purple and crimson draperies upon the ground from the palace to the chariot to demonstrate publicly before men and gods just what sort of man Agamemnon really is: so wanton and glory-seeking that he is willing to trample on lovely things — now draperies, but ten years earlier, his daughter Iphigenia. (This is not a "red carpet" treatment. A carpet is something people are expected to step

upon; precious draperies are not.) Clytemnestra coaxes
Agamemnon to step upon the draperies and walk the
crimson path from the chariot to the palace.

Agamemnon at first announces that trampling on
lovely things is sacrilegious: "That is for gods. . . . I am
a man, not a god. . . . Different, too, is a doormat from a
drapery" (p. 106). Nonetheless, Agamemnon walks on
the draperies. Clytemnestra thereby demonstrates that
Agamemnon will do anything to satisfy his "unbridled
ambition" (p. 53). The chorus watches in horror.

Clytemnestra prays to Zeus that vengeance will be accomplished. Agamemnon and Clytemnestra enter the
palace.

ACT THREE
Act Three begins a few moments after Clytemnestra
and Agamemnon enter the palace. The chorus expresses
fear of impending doom.

Clytemnestra emerges from the palace and tries to
coax Cassandra to enter the palace, ostensibly to prepare
for religious rites "with all the other slaves" (p. 118), but
Cassandra remains immobile. Clytemnestra angrily enters
the palace alone. The chorus, through kind words, per-
suades Cassandra to descend from the chariot.

Cassandra appeals to Apollo to tell her about the
doom to which he has led her. She then recounts to the
chorus bits and snatches of Thyestes' feast. The members
of the chorus are amazed at her knowledge of this event
because she comes from an alien land. They are convinced she is worthy of her great reputation as a prophet,
even though she is recounting something from the past.
Cassandra then predicts the future: Clytemnestra will
murder Agamemnon and Cassandra herself. The chorus
does not believe her and condemns prophecy as evil.

Cassandra explains how she became the prophet of the
god Apollo: Apollo promised that if she made love with
him, he would give her the gift of prophecy. She
promised, and Apollo gave her the gift, but then she

broke her promise. Because a god may not take back a gift once given, Apollo, in revenge for Cassandra's broken promise, neutralized his gift to her in a cruel way: whenever she prophesied, no one would believe her.

Cassandra again recounts Thyestes' feast, and again the chorus is amazed. She again predicts that Clytemnestra will kill Agamemnon, and again the chorus does not believe her. She throws down her prophetic staff and rips off her floral necklace. Her prophetic robes fall from her body, as if removed by an invisible force. Still, her gift of prophecy continues. She states in the clearest terms that Agamemnon will die this day, and so will she. The chorus still does not believe her.

Finally she accepts her fate and expresses the futility of prophecy: "What does it matter if people believe me or not? What will be will be" (p. 133). She comments on the pitiful insecurity of the human condition and how death and annihilation can come in an instant: "Good Fortune can be changed by a shadow, and one swipe of a wet sponge can wipe out a picture" (p. 141). In resignation, she enters the palace.

Agamemnon's cries are heard from within the palace. The members of the chorus begin a satirical democratic discussion as to the most reasonable course of action. By the time the chorus members have decided on a plan — sort of — it is too late to be of any use.

The palace doors fly open to reveal the dead bodies of Agamemnon and Cassandra, his corpse in a silver bathtub, hers on the floor beside him. Clytemnestra, splattered with blood, is standing over the corpses. Agamemnon is covered with one of the draperies upon which he recently walked.

Previously, Cassandra had predicted that Agamemnon would be murdered while "delighting in his bath" (p. 124): "He is caught in a net in a tank of water! Now she is goring him! . . . I am talking to you . . . of a murder in a bath" (p. 125). But no one believed her.

Clytemnestra relates how she snared Agamemnon in

his bath by casting a drapery over him like a fishing net:
"As fishermen cast huge, encircling nets, I cast this — my
most treasured drapery — that he might not escape and
prevent his death" (pp. 145–46).

Then, the chorus states twice that while Agamemnon
was confused and effectively immobilized in this snare,
Clytemnestra stabbed him to death: "You were caught in
a spider's web, and you died a shameful death, stabbed
with a dagger as you lay in your bath, by the treacherous
hand of your queen" (pp. 155–56).

Agamemnon's soldiers, hearing news of his murder,
rush to the scene and see their fallen leader. Clytemnestra, by her boldness and courage, wins them over.

Clytemnestra tells the chorus of her joy at seeing
Agamemnon dead and claims that the Demon Vengeance
of the House of Atreus — not she — killed Agamemnon.

The chorus, horrified by Clytemnestra's crimes and
her joy in recounting them, threatens to condemn her.
She says she killed Agamemnon in retaliation for his
killing their daughter Iphigenia. She demands to know
why the chorus did not condemn Agamemnon for murdering Iphigenia. They have no answer. (Curiously, as
brave and bold as many of the chorus members are, at no
time do they accuse Clytemnestra of killing Agamemnon
because she has a lover, Aegisthus. Their silence on this
matter does not mean, however, that Clytemnestra's love
for Aegisthus was not another reason for her killing
Agamemnon.)

Ironically, Clytemnestra, paragon of vengeance, gives
a touching picture of pure forgiveness when she describes
the reunion of Iphigenia and Agamemnon in the underworld: Iphigenia "will run to greet her father . . . and
throw her arms around him and kiss him" (p. 158).

The prophet Calchas delivers the Victor Today —
Vanquished Tomorrow speech (pp. 158–59) that reiterates the theme of the play — vengeance for vengeance,
blood for blood. He points out the dilemma facing people: on the one hand, "this truth stands eternal at the

throne of God: 'Whoever does evil must pay'" (p. 159). But on the other hand, "Justice is impossible to attain" (p. 159) because where there is vengeance for vengeance, the chain of blood for blood can never be broken, and such "justice" will end up by destroying humanity: "Humanity is destined for destruction" (p. 159). Clytemnestra, hitherto contemptuous of the prophet (it was Calchas whose prophecy resulted in the sacrifice of Iphigenia), agrees with this prophecy and says to him sarcastically, "For once you've predicted the future!" (p. 159).

Aegisthus, Thyestes' son, appears in the courtyard from outside the palace compound. Only a baby when he went into exile with his father, he is now a grown man and Clytemnestra's lover. He recounts his joy at seeing Agamemnon dead and states that his death is retribution for Thyestes' feast, which he describes in detail. He boasts of plotting Agamemnon's murder but admits he had no part in carrying it out. That was done entirely by Clytemnestra.

The chorus accuses Aegisthus of cowardice and licentiousness: instead of going to Troy to fight with the other young men, Aegisthus waited out the war in Agamemnon's palace and bed, all the while plotting Agamemnon's death but not having the courage to kill him.

The chorus begins a small insurrection that is quickly put down by the soldiers recently loyal to Agamemnon, now loyal to Clytemnestra and Aegisthus. The chorus, still defiant, prays that Orestes will return to set things right.

Clytemnestra tells the chorus members to accept their fate, which means accepting her continuing reign of tyranny. Clytemnestra and Aegisthus enter the palace.

The chorus looks on in despair as darkness descends.

AGAMEMNON

CHARACTERS

SENTRY

CHORUS — *elders, with three principals*:

    LEADER

    PROPHET

    NARRATOR

CLYTEMNESTRA — *queen of Argos*

AEGISTHUS — *cousin of* AGAMEMNON
    and lover of CLYTEMNESTRA

HERALD

AGAMEMNON — *king of Argos*

CASSANDRA — *oracle of Apollo; a princess of Troy,*
    daughter of the late Priam, king of Troy;
    sister of the late Paris, a prince of Troy;
    now captive, slave, and mistress of AGAMEMNON

CLYTEMNESTRA'S ATTENDANTS

SOLDIERS — *Greeks returning in victory from Troy*
    on the same ship as AGAMEMNON

SCENE: *Argos, Greece, in front of the palace of* AGAMEM-
NON, *the king, high on a hill overlooking the sea. Mt.*
Arachneos is centered in the near distance before the sea.

    The three major elements of the set, all upstage, are
the palace porch, stage right; the palace terrace, stage
center; and the city walls and city gates, stage left. The
porch and terrace are in the Minoan-Mycenaean style.
The city walls are made of massive blocks of stone. The
palace courtyard is downstage. In a Greek theater, the
palace courtyard would be in the orchestra.

The palace terrace has two steps leading up to it from the courtyard.   Four columns, one at each of the four corners of the terrace, support a roof over it and define it.

The palace porch has six steps leading up to it from the courtyard and two columns supporting its roof.

The palace doors are a few feet deep within the porch. These doors are almost actors. Throughout the play, they open and close without visible assistance, as if they had a life of their own. They are closed at the onset of the play.

A pair of draperies hangs behind the palace doors and serves as a secondary door. Their appearance is described in the stage directions on page 41.   They are closed at the onset of the play.

A hall, which represents the palace interior, is behind the palace doors and draperies. The hall is not visible at the beginning of the play because the doors and the draperies are closed.   When they are open, the hall should be visible from all seats in the theater because essential action takes place there. Visibility is not possible from the extreme side seats of an ancient Greek theater. This problem was solved in antiquity by the use of a device called an eccyclema, *a low, wheeled platform that could be advanced and retracted.*

Additional draperies decorate the walls of the hall. All the draperies are essential to the action of the play.

TIME: *About 1200 B.C., ten years after the onset of the Trojan War (about the same time as the reign of King David in Jerusalem).*

LIGHTING: *The text describes fair weather throughout the play, day and night.   The lighting, whatever special effects are used, should always take this into consideration. The fair weather contrasts with the dark moods and horrifying events.*

MUSIC: *Flutists, drummers, trumpeters.*

MASKS: *Masks are not necessary for a modern perfor-*
mance in which women play women's roles and there are
sufficient actors to play all the parts. Masks, nonetheless,
are highly effective in enhancing dramatic power. They
show that this is an ancient play and they impart a touch
of fear, an emotion that pervades the play.

Domino or half-masks are more effective than Greek
or full masks for characters with speaking parts because
full masks disguise who is speaking and muffle speech,
two undesirable features. Greek masks, however, are
highly effective for the pantomimed parts, such as the two
eagles, the hare, Iphigenia, and others.

ACTS: *Act One*: *A starry night shortly before dawn.*
   Act Two: *Several weeks later —*
       the afternoon of a beautiful day.
   Act Three: *Slightly later the same day.*

PROLOGUE

NARRATOR: The play you are about to see, *AGAMEMNON*, was written in Greek in the fifth century B.C. It is the masterpiece of Aeschylus, who was the first playwright and the father of Western drama. Therefore, from the historical point of view alone, *AGAMEMNON* is unequaled in importance to the theater. In addition, *AGAMEMNON* continues to speak to us because we are still struggling with the timeless issues it presents, including murder, vengeance, justice, unbridled ambition, greed, love, the role of women, religion, reason versus destiny, and war and its consequences.

AGAMEMNON is the first of three plays about the family of King Atreus. Atreus, father of Agamemnon and king of Greece, was challenged in his rule by his brother Thyestes, who also made love to Atreus' wife. Enraged, Atreus banished Thyestes.

In time, Thyestes returned, begging forgiveness. Atreus pretended to forgive him but prepared a horrible revenge. Atreus invited Thyestes to a banquet of reconciliation, but the roast Atreus served Thyestes was the flesh of Thyestes' own children. On discovering the gruesome nature of the feast, Thyestes placed a curse upon the House of Atreus and returned to exile with his one surviving child, the infant Aegisthus.

More than ten years before our play begins, the sons of Atreus, Menelaus and Agamemnon, were ruling together as joint kings of Greece. The

wife of Menelaus, the beautiful Helen, ran away to
the wealthy foreign city of Troy with its handsome
young prince Paris.

Agamemnon raised a mighty Greek army to
sail to Troy to recapture Helen for Menelaus, to
plunder the city's riches, to destroy it, and to win
glory for himself.   But when a violent storm
struck, making sailing impossible, Agamemnon
was told by Calchas the prophet that he must sacrifice his daughter Iphigenia to the goddess Artemis
to obtain fair weather and favorable winds. Driven
by unbridled ambition, Agamemnon sacrificed
Iphigenia.   The storm subsided, favorable winds
followed, and the Greek army sailed to Troy.

Meanwhile, in Greece, Agamemnon's queen,
Clytemnestra, enraged over the death of their
daughter Iphigenia, plotted revenge against
Agamemnon. During the ten-year war, she ruled
cruelly and took a lover, none other than
Aegisthus, the sole surviving brother of the children who were eaten.   Aegisthus, having sworn
vengeance on Agamemnon for Thyestes' feast
prepared by Agamemnon's father, helped
Clytemnestra plot revenge.

Our play, *AGAMEMNON*, begins in Greece
immediately after the carnage that was the fall of
Troy.

ACT ONE

It is shortly before dawn. The black night sky is filled with stars. The SENTRY *is sitting on the terrace. He is facing the palace of* AGAMEMNON, *his back leaning against a column. His profile is silhouetted against the background of the starry sky and the distant mountain.*

SENTRY: (*After a moment, he begins to sing, whistle, or hum a sad tune; then he yawns and stretches. Soft lights come up, faintly illuminating the scene.*)

1[1]

O gods! Give me rest!
Year after year
I've been a watchdog
for the House of Atreus.
And I'm tired of it.

(*Facing the palace, he rolls over on his stomach and assumes the regal posture of a watchdog at rest: forearms parallel, pronated, and palms flush against the ground; elbows each forming a right angle; and chest, head, and neck erect. He maintains this position but turns his head to face the audience and speak.*)

Lying on my elbows,
in the shelter[2] of the palace
of the sons of Atreus,
I have come to know by heart
all the constellations
of the stars of night.

(*maintaining the watchdog posture, but turning his head momentarily toward the stars upstage, then back to the audience*)
Some bring snow, some bring heat.
Brilliant royal families —
stars shining in the skies —
some set, new ones rise.

(*standing, moving downstage from the terrace, then turning and pointing upstage to the distant mountain*)
I watch for that beacon,
that blaze of fire,
to carry forth from Troy
news shouting of her capture.

(*moving to the courtyard, coming downstage, stopping, then speaking confidentially to the audience*)
A woman with a man's mind
but a woman's expectant heart
ordered me to do this.
You see,
a woman is master here.

(*walking back onto the terrace*)
I wander about each night
(*wandering about*)
and lie here and there
(*pointing left and right*)
on this dew-drenched bed,
not even dreams for company.

Fear forever takes the place of sleep.
I cannot close my eyes and rest.
What comforts me?
What heals my lack of sleep?

I sing!
And sometimes I whistle.

(*walking down from the terrace and irrev-
erently sitting down on the palace steps*)
Yes! I sing —
but not a happy song.
I weep in pity for this House,
no longer, as in former days,
ruled like a house of kings.

20   Tonight may I find
an end to my drudgery!

(*pointing to the distant mountain*)
May the fire of good news
burn in the black!

(*Suddenly, the* SENTRY *stands frozen as he
continues to gaze at the mountain. On its
top, a flickering orange light slowly grows
brighter and then bursts into flames.*

    *He runs onto the terrace, stops in his
tracks, gazes intently at the bright beacon,
and with trembling arm points to it and
speaks in great excitement.*)

Look there! (*still pointing*)
A fire in the dark!

(*joyfully*)
Promise of a bright new day
with dancing and singing
for all the people of Argos!

(*running from the terrace down to the
courtyard, then up the palace steps and
across the porch, then pounding on the*

palace doors)
Awake, O Agamemnon's queen!
Quick! Rise from your bed!
Spread the good tidings of this beacon!

(*pounding on the doors again, louder
than before*)
The messenger is here!
The shining flare proclaims:

(*He quickly creates a megaphone with his
hands.   Then, facing the audience, he
slowly sweeps his head through nearly
180 degrees as he slowly shouts his as-
tounding message.*)

"Troy is taken!"

(*running down the palace steps into the
courtyard, joyously*)
I'll start my dance right now,
for my lord's dice well cast
make me a winner, too!
And he has thrown triple sixes!

(*He does a short dance to a cheerful version of the sad tune he was singing at the
beginning of the play.   Then he stops
short; his mood changes abruptly, and he
prays solemnly.*)

May the king come home,
and may I clasp within my own
the hand of the master I love.

(*in confidence, to the audience*)
Other things I leave unsaid.
An ox sits on my tongue!

If the palace walls had a voice,
they'd tell the story
loud and clear.

(*continuing in confidence*)
I speak freely
to those who understand.
But to those who don't —
well, I don't remember!

(*His dance resumes, faster than before,
and, whistling his joyous tune, he runs
through the terrace and exits.*)

(*The palace doors open.
A pair of draperies drawn across the
doorway blocks the view into the palace.
The draperies are purple and crimson,
with highly visible and pleasing patterns.
They are woven loosely, like fishnet, but
they have a few widely spaced bands of
tightly woven fabric [see notes 24–25].*

CLYTEMNESTRA'S ATTENDANTS *part the
draperies and reveal more draperies
hanging on the walls of the hall. The* AT-
TENDANTS *emerge from the palace and
perform a dance of celebration while
lighting torches in the courtyard and oil
lamps on the terrace. When the dance is
over, they run back into the palace.
The palace doors close.*)

(*The members of the* CHORUS *enter the
courtyard from all sides and assume positions throughout the courtyard and terrace. [Henceforth, the word "courtyard"
will be understood to include the terrace.]*

They stare at the torches and lamps and each other with agitation and puzzlement.

Most of the time, each member of the CHORUS *speaks individually and speaks only one stanza; then another member of the* CHORUS *speaks the next stanza, and the members of the* CHORUS *continue in a chain. Separate stanzas are indicated by space between the lines. A stanza may be several lines long or as short as one line.*

From time to time, the CHORUS *speaks in unison, but only for one stanza. Speech in unison is indicated in the stage directions at the beginning of the appropriate stanza and ends at the end of that stanza. At the onset of the subsequent stanza, the members of the* CHORUS *revert to speaking as individuals although there are no stage directions, apart from these, to indicate this.*

Additionally, the three major CHORUS *members, the* LEADER, *the* PROPHET, *and the* NARRATOR, *have major roles in the play and speeches designated specifically for them. These speeches are indicated as they are for any other character.*

The members of the CHORUS *do not stand stiffly like columns and deliver formal recitations. They are players and dancers who move meaningfully about the courtyard, singly or in groups, coming together or dispersing, grouping and regrouping in accordance with the context of the lines, and gesturing and pantomiming accordingly. Only a few specific stage directions are henceforth provided.*)

40   LEADER: (*downstage*)

Ten long years ago
the great kings of Greece
went to war
against the king of Troy.

CHORUS: One thousand ships
sailed from our shore
with an army of Greeks —
their commanders in chief,
Menelaus and Agamemnon,

brothers ruling together,
prize team,
divine kings,

(*in unison*)
mighty sons of Atreus.

Shrill and angry their cry of war,
like vultures shrieking in grief
over stolen young.

High above the mountain nest they fly,
circle and wheel,
bank and swoop.

What good to have tended the nest
now that the fledglings are gone?

Still, some god in heaven,
Apollo, Pan, or Zeus,[3]
hears the wail,
so thin and high,
of these travelers of the sky,
and sends,
sooner or later,

(*in unison*)

Furies against the transgressors.

59   And so it was
when Almighty Zeus,
great God of Hospitality,
sent the sons of Atreus
against Paris, prince of Troy.

All those battles
for the sake of one whore!

All those muscles aching
and spears broken
and knees ground in dust!
Greek and Trojan
have it alike.

No matter how things are going now,
the end depends on Destiny.

Neither sacrifices,
whether burnt
or unburnt,
nor libations,
nor tears
can soften
the inexorable anger of God.[4]

We are old,
and thereby dishonored,
completely cast off
from young men
and their battles.

Instead,
(*in unison*)
we stay at home.

(*those members of the* CHORUS *with walking sticks*)
Weak as children,
we prop ourselves on canes.

Energetic little boys,
so eager, so willing,
are weak as old men
and not ready for war,

(*those members of the* CHORUS *with walking sticks*)
while we who are old
go about on three feet,
no stronger than children,
withered leaves,
drifting about,
daydreaming.

(*The palace doors open. After a moment,*
CLYTEMNESTRA, *almost like a specter, slowly parts the draperies and steps through
them onto the porch. She moves to the
head of the staircase and surveys the* CHO-
RUS, *moving her head slowly from side to
side while her body remains erect and motionless. All eyes turn to her, but she does
not respond.*)

83   LEADER: But you, our lady,
Clytemnestra,
our queen,
daughter of Tyndareus,
What is happening?
What news have you heard?

CHORUS: Why do you light
sacred fires to the gods

everywhere?

The altars to all the gods —
those in heaven and
those in the underworld,
those protecting the city
and those in the marketplace —
are ablaze.

Here
(*pointing to the torches in the courtyard*)
torch flames rise sky high,

while there
(*pointing to the lamps on the terrace*)
offerings flicker softly —
sacred mixtures
of meal and honey and oil,
treasures taken
from the cool cellars of kings —
soothing and comforting
like a pure salve or drug
that takes away pain.

(*in unison*)
What does all this mean?

Heal my anxious heart!
One minute
I sink into blackest thought.
The next,
sweet hope
shining in those flames
wards off the pain
eating at my heart.

(CLYTEMNESTRA *slowly turns and reenters
the palace. The doors close behind her.*)

104   PROPHET : I am a master
                 at chanting prophecies[5a]
                 of wondrous journeys and victories
                 coming to kings.
                 And, old as I am,
                 by God's grace,
                 I can do it still.
                 The power of prophecy
                 surges within me.

                 That same power
                 let me interpret
                 the omen of the birds[5b]
                 and send the brother-kings,
                 lords of the youth of Greece,
                 with a single heart,
                 stout spear in strong hand,
                 on to the land of Troy[5c]
                 to seek Vengeance.

                 Two eagles,
                 kings of birds —
                 omen for kings of ships[5d] —
                 one all black,
                 the other tail-feathers of white,
                 alighted on the right,
                 the spear-hand side,
                 of the palace.

                 Then, watched by all,
                 they caught a hare
                 as she ran for the last time.
                 Pregnant and bursting with unborn young,
                 she was ripped wide open![5e]

121   CHORUS : (*in unison*)
                 Sing sorrow, sorrow,

but hope that all
turns out for the best.

NARRATOR: The trusted prophet of the army
understood the omen.

PROPHET: Here is my interpretation:[6a]
Not two birds,
but the two warrior sons of Atreus —
the leaders of the army —
were feeding on that hare![6b]
All in good time
this carnage shall take place in Troy.[6c]
But before then, within her walls,
the Fates shall send
a plague upon her cattle.

May the gods not crash
a hammer of wrath
down upon our Greek soldiers,
mighty sword forged against Troy,
and dash it to pieces
before it strikes its goal.

The virgin Artemis is angry[6d]
at the flying hounds of her father
for eating the unborn hares
and their quivering mother.
She hates the eagles' feast.[6e]

139   CHORUS: (*in unison*)
Sing sorrow, sorrow,
but hope that all
turns out for the best.

PROPHET: Lovely Artemis,
caring and kind
to the tender cubs

of ferocious lions,
has sympathy
for sucklings
of all the wild beasts
that roam the wilderness.

O Apollo, the physician!
Grant meaning to this omen
that seems good as well as evil.
Do not let Artemis
punish the Greeks[7a]
with endless foul winds,
making sailing impossible,[7b]
forcing another unholy sacrifice,
bringing men meat
they must not eat,
and creating family strife,
breaking the bond
between husband and wife.

(The palace doors slowly open. As before,
CLYTEMNESTRA *slowly parts the draperies,*
steps forward onto the porch, walks to the
head of the staircase, and scans the CHO-
RUS.)

NARRATOR: Wrath keeps house here.
Fearful, cunning,
she appears unexpectedly,
watching, waiting,
remembering a child
that must be avenged.

(After a moment, from within the palace,
AEGISTHUS *slowly parts the draperies, steps*
forward onto the porch, walks to the head
of the staircase, and scans the CHORUS.
AEGISTHUS *places one arm around*

CLYTEMNESTRA *'s waist, and with his free hand takes one of her hands and kisses it. They smile at each other and press cheeks with the comfort and familiarity of established lovers.   Then they disengage.* AEGISTHUS *surveys the crowd with a smirk and enters the palace.*

CLYTEMNESTRA *lingers a moment, scans the crowd, then also enters the palace. The doors close. The* CHORUS *resumes.*)

NARRATOR: Although Calchas
spoke of good things, too,
it was these fatal signs
from the birds
to the House of the kings,
spoken with such feeling,
that struck me most.

CHORUS: (*in unison*)
Sing sorrow, sorrow,
but hope that all
turns out for the best.

160   LEADER: (*turning to heaven*)
O Zeus![8a]
I don't even know
if this name of invocation
pleases You!
Whatever You are,
I call You by that name!

I have pondered everything.
(*to the* CHORUS *and the audience*)
Discard vain sorrows
from your thoughts,
for nothing compares to Zeus!

The first god of heaven —
Uranus is his name —
once was great,
"Unconquerable!"
he used to boast,
but now he is
as if he never was.

His son and successor —
Cronus is his name —
found his master
in his own son, Zeus,
and now Cronus
also goes unsung.

Oh, the Victory of Zeus![8b]
Let us shout it aloud
with all our might,
the Victory that teaches men
everything there is to know —
the Victory that blazed
the path to understanding,
the Victory that fixed the law
that Wisdom comes through suffering.

Fate sharpens her knives
upon the human heart.
Even as we sleep,
our tears from other days
drip, drip upon the hone.
And from our pain,
inflicted from heaven's high throne,
comes a divine gift —
Wisdom.[8c]

NARRATOR: (*The rest of the* CHORUS *pantomimes with dance accompanied by music.*)

183

On that day,
Agamemnon,
the elder king,
commander in chief
of the Greek ships,
did not blame prophets.
The foul wind
was caused by Bad Luck.[9]

No ship sailed,
provisions failed,
and the Greek army
hungered at Aulis,
across the straits
from the shores at Chalcis,[10]
while roaring tides
with crashing waves
ebbed and flowed,
and the north wind blew
from Strymon.

Ships kept at anchor
brought boredom
and restlessness.
A foul wind tugs and pulls at men
as well as hull and line.
And delay heaped upon delay
wore down the youth of Argos.

Then, to calm the wind,
the prophet,
blaming Artemis,
proposed another means,
worse than the bitter storm.[11]

Agamemnon the king
dashed his scepter
to the ground

and could not contain
a flood of tears.

205   Agamemnon
spoke these words:

"Fate will be angry
if I do not obey,
and angry
if I sacrifice this child,
the beauty of my house,
and at the altar,
with my own child's blood,
stain these father's hands.
Whatever I do is wrong![12a]

"Yet, how can I fail
fleet and friends?
They urge sacrifice
of innocent blood,
and that is just.[12b]

"May all turn out for the best."

You see!
He blamed it all on Fate!
Look how unbridled ambition
twisted his mind!

Evil of evils,
when Daring throws Reason
to the winds!
Now his will
would stop at nothing.[13a]

The sickness in men's minds,
bringing Daring out of the blue,
is the very source of woe.

(The CHORUS *pantomimes the sacrifice of
Iphigenia from here to the end of the* NAR-
RATOR*'s speech.)*

And so,
to assure strength
in a war waged for a woman,
Agamemnon took it upon himself
to make his daughter
the first sacrifice
for the sake of ships![13b]

226   The child's pleas
and cries of "Father!"
were in vain.

What good are tears
when kings are bent on battle?

The father prayed.
Then he gave the command
that she be lifted aloft,
dressed in sacrificial robes,
above the altar —
like a goat for sacrifice!

Her sweet lips gagged,
her speech stifled,
she could not curse
the House of Atreus.

The picture is still fresh
in my mind!

Her saffron robe
fell streaming to the ground.

The look in her eyes
wounded her executioners
like arrows.

She tried to speak.
Many a time on other days
she chanted in worship
at the festive table of her father.
And over the third cup of wine,[14]
dedicated to Zeus our Savior,
in the clear voice of a child
filled with purest love,
she chanted a hymn.

248   I could not watch
what happened next,
and I cannot bear
to talk about it.[15]

But the art of Calchas
never fails.

LEADER: Justice has decreed
that Wisdom comes through suffering.

CHORUS: Never seek to know the future
ahead of time.
It is grief given too soon.

(*in unison*)
All will come clear
in the early morning's light.

(*A soft, blue-white light begins to suffuse
the black night sky and gradually grows
in intensity. The stars begin to fade. The
sea is now clearly visible in the distance.
Dawn is breaking.   The bonfire on the*

mountaintop is still burning brightly.
    The palace doors open. CLYTEMNES-
TRA *parts the draperies and walks across
the porch to the head of the stairs. The
doors close. She turns stage left and walks
to the edge of the porch, where she stands
and gazes at the beacon and the dawn.
She is mesmerized. The* LEADER *turns to
address her, but she does not respond.*)

LEADER: May all things turn out well,
        as you desire,
        sole guardian,
        mighty fortress of
        our beloved homeland.

        I revere you, Clytemnestra,
        and your power.
        When the king is gone
        and his throne is vacant,
        the queen rules,
        and all honor must be given her.

        Is it good news or bad
        that makes you light sacred fires
        to the gods?
        I wish to know,
        (*suddenly timidly*)
        but I understand
        should you choose not to tell.

        (*Dawn continues to break. The band of
        sky nearest the earth turns violet, then
        rose, then orange, while the remainder of
        the sky is turning bright blue.*)

264   CLYTEMNESTRA: (*ecstatic and amazed, turning
        from the beacon to the* CHORUS *and almost*

running to the head of the staircase)
It's true!
Just like the proverb!
"Good news comes
when Mother Night
is giving birth to dawn."

You are about to know joy
beyond all you ever hoped to know.

Our Greeks have taken Troy!

LEADER: What are you saying?
Words too good to be true!

CLYTEMNESTRA: The Greeks have taken Troy.
Is that not clear?

CHORUS: I'm beginning to see,
and my eyes fill with tears of joy.

CLYTEMNESTRA: Your eyes reveal a loyal heart.

CHORUS: How can we be sure?
Is there a sign?

CLYTEMNESTRA: There is.
There is no doubt about it —
unless a god has tricked me.

CHORUS: What is it then?
Do you have faith in dreams,
believable though they are?

CLYTEMNESTRA: I take nothing
from a brain
dull with sleep.

CHORUS: Then has some rumor
            charmed you —
            awakened your hope?

CLYTEMNESTRA : What do you take me for —
            a young girl with silly thoughts?

LEADER: When was the citadel stormed?

CLYTEMNESTRA : Last night,
            now giving birth to dawn.

280   CHORUS: What kind of messenger
            comes in speed like that?

CLYTEMNESTRA : (*Descending the palace steps, she
            walks across the courtyard to stage
            center.*)

            The God of Fire
            sent the bright light
            from Mount Ida near Troy;
            and fire after fire,
            relaying the torch,
            carried it here.

            (*In this exciting Beacon speech,
            CLYTEMNESTRA explains that the message
            of Greece's victory over Troy has traveled
            from Troy to Greece by a relay of light
            from eight beacons. As she mentions each
            beacon station, she points upstage to its
            position far across the sea, beginning up-
            stage left and swinging across to upstage
            right, then reversing direction to end at
            upstage center on Mt. Arachneos.
                She points as if she can see the bea-
            cons with her very own eyes. With the*

*clever use of lighting, the audience should
actually be able to see them, too.*

CLYTEMNESTRA *speaks with excitement,
as if describing a race in progress, but she
does not speak quickly. She speaks clearly and emphasizes every station.*

*To be most effective, each beacon
should   light   immediately   before*
CLYTEMNESTRA *points to it, and all the
beacons should be in front of the audience. The final (and closest) beacon, on
Mt. Arachneos, should be a continuous
distant bonfire. The others, visible only in
her imagination, should be momentary
points of flashing light.*

CLYTEMNESTRA *'s description closely
parallels the geography in the "Map of
Agamemnon's World," pp. 172–73. The
following diagram represents the progres-
sion of the beacons across the stage:*

#6   #5   #4   #3   #2   #1
              #7

                   Sky

                   Sea

                   #8
              Mt. Arachneos

              (UPSTAGE)

Palace porch; Terrace   City walls
(stage right)   (stage left)
                   Courtyard
              (DOWNSTAGE)

CLYTEMNESTRA : (*turning and pointing upstage left beyond the sea toward Beacon #1 at Troy*)
From Ida

(*turning one-fifth of the way [about 35 degrees] toward stage right, then pointing toward Beacon #2*)
to the rock of Hermes
on the isle of Lemnos,

(*turning another fifth [35 degrees] toward upstage right, then pointing toward Beacon #3*)
to the third station —
the heights of Zeus on Athos —
the great torch ran on.

(*scanning upward*)
Then, leaping into the sky
and vaulting over the sea,
the torch raced mightily onward
and joyously.

Pine timbers
burst into flaming gold
like a sunrise
and carried the bright message

(*turning another fifth [35 degrees] toward upstage right, then pointing toward Beacon #4*)
to the sentinel cliffs of Macistos.
The fire,
never slowing down,
nor taking time to sleep,
relayed the torch
in the courier chain.

Far across Euripus' straits
the shining light sped on

(*turning another fifth [35 degrees] toward*
upstage right, then pointing toward Bea-
con #5)
to sentries at Messapion
who, kindling high-piled silvery brush,
passed the message on.

The fire, never growing dim,
grew ever brighter.
Shining like the full moon,
the brilliant light leaped over
the valley of Asopos,

(*turning the last fifth [35 degrees] to ex-*
treme stage right)
onward to the cliffs of Cithaeron,
and wakened the next station of the torch,
where sentries,
knowing how far the blaze had run,
(*pointing toward Beacon #6*)
kindled another beacon
greater than commanded.

(*scanning upward*)
The light leaped high
above Gorgopis marsh —
how it was reflected! —

(*reversing direction and turning back to-*
ward stage left a quarter of the way [45
degrees])
and,
striking Aegyplanctus mountaintop,
the fire did not linger.

302

(*pointing toward Beacon #7*)
Kindled once more,
the great light sped on.

(*scanning upward*)
Like a shooting star,
the gigantic fire
passed far beyond
the promontory
of the Saronic Gulf,
until it swooped downward
and landed,
at last, nearby,

(*turning to upstage center, then pointing
to Beacon #8 on Mt. Arachneos*)
on the high peak of Mt. Arachneos,
our watchtower.

From there,
a fire fathered by a blaze at Ida

(*pointing to all the torches ablaze and all
the lamps flickering in the courtyard*)
inflamed the House of Atreus.

In this way
my torchlight messengers,
one after another,
completed the designated course.

To the first runner
and to the last
goes the victory![16]

And that is how
my lord at Troy
sent this message

home to me.

(By the time CLYTEMNESTRA *has concluded this speech, the entire sky is blue. The stars have faded and disappeared, but the bonfire on Mt. Arachneos is shining more brightly than ever, as if it has replaced the sun. It is a new day.)*

LEADER: The gods, my lady,
will shortly have my prayers
and thanksgivings.
For now,
I am numb,
struck dumb.
Please,
tell the story again.

320   CLYTEMNESTRA: The Greeks have taken Troy
on this very day!

I can see it now:

The city echoes
with a clash of cries.
Pour oil and vinegar
into the same bowl.
They do not mix like friends,
but join in battle.
And so it is
with victors and vanquished
by the very opposition
of their fates.

This very moment
Trojan women
stoop to gather in their arms
dead husbands and brothers.

Children reach out
to cling to dead mothers,
and cry at the death
of those most dear
from lips
that will never again
be free.

Now that the fighting is over,
the Greeks,
too keyed up this night to sleep,
hunger for breakfast —
such as that city can provide.

Fortune, and not a general,
and not a king,
makes all the necessary arrangements.

Ah, I can see them now:

Greek men are going to sleep
in Trojan homes
their spears have taken.
Sheltered from open sky
and frost
and damp of evening,
no sentries set,
they sleep the sleep of bliss
the whole night through.

338

Oh, may they respect
the gods of that nation
and all the holy temples
of the captured land
so that they, the victors,
will not be vanquished in turn!

Let not greed
and desire to make their victory
more complete
overcome these men!
Let them not ravage
what must not be ravaged!

For they still have ahead
the run to safety and to home.
They have passed the halfway mark,
but they still must run
the homestretch
in their course.

And even if our army
comes home without offending gods,
still, the anger of the massacred
may never go to sleep.

Oh, let there be no new wrong done!

These are my thoughts —
only a woman's.

May Good triumph,
and may all of us live to see it.

That is my sincerest wish.

351   LEADER: My lady, no wise man
could have spoken better.
I have heard your tale
and do believe it.
Now I shall make
thanksgiving to the gods,
who have given us this magnificent gift
to replace our misery.

(CLYTEMNESTRA *turns from the* LEADER
and walks toward the palace. She as-
cends the stairs. When she reaches the top
of the staircase, the palace doors open.
She crosses the porch and enters the
palace. The palace doors close.

All the while, the members of the CHO-
RUS *remain motionless except for their*
heads and eyes, which have been follow-
ing CLYTEMNESTRA . *After the palace doors*
close, the CHORUS *turns to the audience.*)

CHORUS : (*in unison, joyfully*)
Past sorrow
turns to present joy.

(*with pantomime and dance, accompa-*
nied by music)
O Zeus, our Lord!
O loving Night!
To give to the Greeks such glory!

(*solemnly*)
You cast over the battlements of Troy
a net of no escape
for great and small alike —
enormous meshwork of slavery
and absolute disaster.

I tremble before Zeus,
God of the Host
and God of the Guest,
who extracted from Paris
such payment.

Carefully Zeus drew the bow,
slowly,
that the arrow

365

would not fall short of the mark
nor overshoot the stars.

(*in unison*)
The retribution of Zeus!
He acted as He decreed.

A man dared to think
the gods would not punish him
for trampling down
on sacred, lovely things.

(*in unison*)
That man had no fear of God.

The curse of unbridled Daring is clear:
Ruin is the reward
for reckless crimes of rich men
abounding in wealth
yet greedy for more.

Wealth without tears —
just enough —
the wise man asks no more.
A man with a good share
of common sense
has plenty!

Gold is poor armor
for the man
who spurns the high altar of justice.

He is forced on and on
by relentless Temptation,
the calculating child
of absolute Ruin.

(*in unison*)

There is no cure for this disease!

Wickedness has no place to hide.

Crime does not smolder,
but burns flagrantly and malignantly!

Cheap bronze, when tested,
turns to everlasting blackness.

Such a man, when tested,
proves himself as vain as any child
who tries to catch a bird in flight.

He heaps shame upon himself
and brings disaster to his nation.

What god listens
to this man's prayers?

Whoever turns to ways like these
is struck down in his wickedness.

399   NARRATOR: (*the other members of the* CHORUS *pantomiming*)
Such a one was Paris.
He came as a guest
to the palace of the sons of Atreus —
and stole Helen, the queen, away,
abusing hospitality.

She danced
as she passed through the city gates —
daring beyond daring! —
but brought to Troy her dowry,
Death!

She left behind a people

clamoring for shields
and spears
and sailing ships.

And the prophets of the great House
wept aloud and cried:

"Woe, woe, the palace,
our palace, our king.
Woe, woe, their bed,
worn like a well-trodden path
from all the lovemaking
with her husband."

Menelaus the king
was silent and withdrawn,
grieving and dishonored,
but blaming no one.

The agony of his loss
was there for all to view.

While he pined
for his queen beyond the sea,
a phantom reigned in his house.

Her statues, showing her beauty,
only increased his misery.
For statues have eyes without fire
and cannot make love.

420   Past joys came in dreams,
bringing hollow delight.

It is vain to dream wonderful dreams.
The vision,
slipping from the arm's embrace,
escapes on wings,

gliding down
the corridors of sleep,
never to return again.

LEADER: Those were the troubles
of the king.
But now, throughout all Greece,
are worse troubles still.

CHORUS: (*pantomiming a funeral procession*)
In many a soldier's home,
heartbreak.
Families sent forth living sons,
but now,
in place of those young men,
urns with ashes are carried home.

437   LEADER: The God of War trades bodies
like a merchant trading gold.
The balance of the battle
pivots on his spear.
And from corpse-fires at Ilium,[17]
crating urns with gentle care,
He sends to dear ones,
weeping with bitter tears,
the dust of ashes
that once were men.

CHORUS: Through lamentation
comes their praise:

"How well your son
did fight at Troy!"

"How bravely our son died"

"— in the slaughter!"

"— for someone else's woman!"

This they whisper in secret.

But anger
at the sons of Atreus
and their quarrel
slowly creeps
from beneath their grief:

"There, by the walls of Ilium,
our beautifully built young men
lie in graves,
deep in the alien soil
of the land they hated
and conquered."

456   The citizens speak,
and their voice is filled with hatred.
And the curse of the people
must be paid in full.

(*The members of the* CHORUS *deliver their
lines slowly while dancing one at a time,
in slow motion, from the periphery to center stage. Upon reaching their assigned
positions, they freeze. The result is that
the members of the* CHORUS *form a low,
broad triangle like statues in a pediment
of a Greek temple, with peripheral figures
of the triangle lying on the ground, the
central figure standing, and intermediate
figures crouching and kneeling.*)

I am afraid.

What is lurking
in the gloom?

The gods mark
those that massacre.

The dark Furies
stalk the man who wins dishonestly,
reverse his good fortune,
and drop him into obscurity.

Reduced to nothing,
his life is over.
And help is nowhere
to be found.

Too much fame
is a heavy burden.

Zeus' thunderbolts
crash on towering mountains.

Let me attain
no envied wealth.

Let me not plunder nations
only to be taken in turn

(*in unison*)
and be at the mercy
of another's power.

(*All lighting is extinguished.*)

ACT TWO

There is no intermission between Act One and Act Two.

It is several weeks later — the afternoon of a beautiful day. No torches are burning in the courtyard. No beacon is burning on the mountaintop. As the act begins, each member of the CHORUS *is at a peripheral place in the courtyard.*

475 LEADER: Rumor of the light's bright news
flies through the city.
Who knows if it is true?
Perhaps the gods have played a trick.

CHORUS: Childish! Foolish! —
to inflame your hearts
by light of torch
only to weep again
when the story changes
in the end!

How like a woman
to get so excited
because the news is good
and not because it's true.

Women are too quick to believe,
too quick to exaggerate —
and just as quickly
their rumor dies.

LEADER: (*looking in the direction of the sea and
            seeing someone coming*)
            But now we shall know
            the meaning of beacons and torches,
            race courses of flame.
            Now we shall learn
            if this joyous light was real
            or whether, like a dream,
            it kindled our hopes
            while blinding our eyes.

            I see a herald coming from the beach
            with sprigs of olive on his brow
            and dust,
            the dry sister of mud,
            upon his feet.
            I suspect he has a voice
            and can do more
            than kindle flame
            from mountain timber
            and send smoke signals!

            He will tell us
            to rejoice or —
            but I dare not speak the other.
            Things look good.
            May it only be so.
            Let any man who prays otherwise
            be the object of his prayer.

HERALD: (*The* HERALD's *entry is an electrifying
            moment because the* CHORUS *knows that he
            is bringing definitive news of whether Troy
            has truly fallen. The* HERALD *transmits ex-
            citement not only through his words but
            also through his dance, as he runs and
            leaps from one place in the courtyard to
            another and pantomimes his descriptions.*

Each time the HERALD *comes to rest,
the* CHORUS *gathers around him and reacts
to him.   As he begins to move to another
part of the courtyard, the members of the*
CHORUS *disperse, then quickly regroup
around him when he comes to rest at his
new position.   Only a few of the* HERALD*'s
movements are indicated in the stage directions that follow.*

The HERALD *enters through the city
gates, running toward the palace steps.
He falls prone to the ground in front of
the palace and kisses and embraces the
earth.   He stands.   The* LEADER *offers him
a jug of water.   The* HERALD *drinks eager-
ly, then hands the jug back to the* LEADER.
Then the HERALD *speaks in joy and amazement.*)

503   Home! Argos!
           After ten years, home!
           All hope shattered but this!

           And yet,
           I never dared to dream
           that I should die in Argos
           and be buried in beloved soil.

           (*with arms extended and facing heaven*)
           Thank the gods for the land of Argos!
           Thank the gods for the light of day!

           (*nodding to the heavens as if making eye
           contact with Zeus*)
           Oh, many are Your blessings,
           O King of Heaven, O Zeus!

           (*turning his head slightly, as if now mak-*

*ing eye contact with Apollo in another po-
sition in the heavens*)
And you, my lord Apollo!
May it be your will
to end your arrow-storm upon us.
Your wrath was satisfied
by the banks of the river Scamander.
Lord Apollo,
be our Savior and our Healer now!

(*extending his arms widely as if in the
presence of all the gods in heaven*)
O gods assembled, I greet you all! —

(*proudly, smiling broadly*)
and Hermes, beloved herald,
my own patron god,
who decreed all heralds sacred! —

and dear departed ancestors,
and dead heroes,

(*turning to the* CHORUS)
and you, great nation,
that sent forth an army:

(*announcing joyously*)
Good news!
Survivors are coming!

Great hall, beloved palace,
sanctuary of gods
facing the sun,
if ever there was a time
to receive a king
with admiration in your eyes,
it is now!

After so long,
he is coming! —
our king,
523   Agamemnon! —
bringing light to the gloom
of all assembled here.

Greet him with gladness
as he well deserves,
this man who uprooted
and buried Ilium
with the spade of Zeus,
great God of Justice!

Troy's altars and sacred shrines
were turned into the ground,
and all her seeds
were burned and scattered!

He is coming,
our king,
elder son of Atreus,
man honored
above all living men!

Paris and his nation
got just what they deserved.
He was guilty of rape
and theft,
and he was damned.
Now he has lost his captured prize
and mowed down his father's house,
destroying even the earth
on which it stood.
The sons of Priam
have paid twice over
for Paris' terrible sins.

LEADER: (*with open arms to the* HERALD)
            Welcome home, and be glad,
            herald of our army of Greeks!
            (*embracing the* HERALD)

HERALD: (*simultaneously embracing the* LEADER)
            I am glad.
            I no longer ask the gods for death.
            (*separating from the* LEADER *but continuing to face him*)

LEADER: Love of country moved you so?

HERALD: Home! I'm home!
            My eyes fill up with tears of joy.

LEADER: Yours was a sickness
            with a sweet ache.

HERALD: Which sickness is that?

LEADER: Longing for loved ones again.

HERALD: Why, I see you yearned for us
            as much as we for you!

LEADER: So much so
            I used to weep
            within my heart.

HERALD: What caused you such despair?

LEADER: Until now
            silence has been the remedy
            to prevent disaster.

HERALD: But why?
            Whom did you fear

while the king was away?

LEADER: You say you asked the gods for death.
Let us say we did the same.

HERALD: (*to the* CHORUS)
But, as you see,
all has turned out well.
And until now
part of our luck was good,
while part we cursed
over and over again.

(*saluting the gods and smiling*)
But who except the gods
can live life without misfortune?

(*solemnly*)
Were I to tell you
of our misery at sea —
the misfortunes,
the cramped quarters,
the wretched berths! —

(*shrugging his shoulders in resignation,
good-humoredly*)
but then, when didn't
we complain about something?

(*solemnly*)
Ashore it was worse:
We had to sleep against
the enemy ramparts.
Drizzle from the sky
and dew from the earth
drenched and ruined our clothes
and filled our hair with lice.

560

And the winters
beyond endurance —
the blizzards from Mount Ida
when all the birds died.

And the summers —
the noonday sun,
so hot, oppressive,
the sea deathly still
beneath a windless sky.

But why relive our grief?

(*emphatically*)
It's over for us
and over for those who died
and never again will rise or care!

Why must the living recount
the tales of the dead?
Why suffer through
the same bad fortune twice?

Good-bye to all unhappiness
once and for all!

(*The* HERALD *and the* CHORUS *freeze.*
     The palace doors open.
     CLYTEMNESTRA *parts the draperies,
steps out onto the porch, and walks to the
head of the staircase. She stares at the*
HERALD *but remains motionless.*
     The palace doors close.
     The HERALD *and the* CHORUS *unfreeze.
The* HERALD *and the* LEADER *do not notice*
CLYTEMNESTRA. *A few members of the* CHO-
RUS *see her, but others are paying atten-
tion only to the* HERALD.)

HERALD: (*emphatically, from downstage center*)
We, the survivors of the Greek army,
have won!
That outweighs our losses.

And here, in broadest daylight,
we whose fame
has flown on wings
over land and sea
can proudly boast:

"There was a time
when the Greeks captured Troy,
and on Greek temples
nailed the spoils —
glory of days gone by!"

(*solemnly*)
And they who hear these things
shall praise this nation
and her leaders.
They shall thank God
and exalt Him.
For He did this.

And there you have the story.

LEADER: (*partially stupefied*)
583   I give in.
Your story has convinced me.
And old people
are always young enough to learn.

Above all others,
Clytemnestra and her house
must hear this news
that makes my life so wonderful!

CLYTEMNESTRA : (*As soon as she begins to speak, the* HERALD, *the* LEADER, *and the members of the* CHORUS, *some of whom are startled to find her present, turn to face her.*)

I cried for joy
some time ago,
when the first herald,
the great torchlight,
spoke of Troy's capture
and overthrow.

Then there were those
who laughed at me and said,
"You trust in bonfires
and believe that Troy has fallen!
How like a woman,
won over by things like that!"
So men spoke.
They thought
I was out of my mind.

Undaunted,
I continued to kindle flames.
Throughout the city,
woman after woman
rejoiced,
gave praise,
and, as women do,
blessed the fragrant flames
in the temples of the gods.

(*to the* HERALD, *disdainfully*)
But why should *you*
tell me the tale at such length,
when I shall hear the story
from my lord himself?

598

(*reflectively*)
For now,
how best to receive my honored lord,
who comes home to me again?
What is sweeter for a wife
than to open wide the gates
before her husband home from war,
saved by the hand of God?

(*to the* HERALD)
Take this message to the king:
"Come as fast as you can
to the city that loves you
and to your queen,
as true today
as the day you left.

(*The members of the* CHORUS *react in dis-belief by glancing at each other knowing-ly, snickering cynically, shaking their heads, rolling their eyes, etc., but the* HER-ALD *is entranced with* CLYTEMNESTRA *.*)

"She has been
the watchdog of the house,
gentle only to the master,
ferocious to his enemies.
She is that sort of woman
who would not break
the seal upon her,
however endless the years.
She has enjoyed
no man's companionship.
She is as free from scandal
and gossip
as she is from knowledge
of coloring bronze."[18]

(*In pantomime she thrusts a knife. Then
she turns abruptly toward the palace. The
palace doors open.* CLYTEMNESTRA *crosses
the palace porch, parts the draperies, and
enters. The doors close.*)

HERALD: (*turning from the palace to the* CHORUS,
         naively)
         Boasting so sincere
         befits a noble queen.

LEADER: She spoke those words for you.
        But if you only knew!

        Now tell me, herald,
        what about Menelaus,
        beloved ruler in this land?
        Is he living, too?
        Has he come home again?

620   HERALD: I don't know how to lie,
               to change bad news
               and make it good for friends.

      LEADER: You have no news
              both good and true?
              Well, you may as well speak.
              There is no way to hide the truth
              when it is not good.

      HERALD: He and his ship disappeared.
              That's no lie.

      LEADER: Did he sail from Troy?
              And did a storm
              that struck you both
              whirl him away?

HERALD: You've scored a direct hit
and made a long, sad story short.

LEADER: (*annoyed at having to work so hard to
get information*)
No news from other sailors?
Is he alive?
Is he dead?

HERALD: Nobody knows
except the Sun,
who gives us life.

LEADER: Tell us about this storm
upon our fleet.
Was it sent
by the wrath of the gods?
How did it end?
How did it begin?

636   HERALD: It is not fitting
to ruin this happy day
with bad news,
which must be kept separate
from thanksgiving
to the gods.

When the messenger of defeat
sadly brings to his country
news it prayed never to hear,
a wound is scored
on the body of the people.
Thereby, many men
who never went to war
are struck
by that two-edged sword
so dear
to the War God's hand.

Double-bladed disaster
strikes twice.
The messenger of gloom
should sing of sorrow
to the Furies,
who find such music
triumphant.

I have told you
the good news
you've longed for.
I have been welcomed
by a joyous nation.
Now, how can I mix
good news with bad
and tell of the storm
on the Greeks,
sent by the wrath of God?

(*solemnly*)
Sea and Fire,
deepest enemies
from ancient times,
did conspire
to blast to pieces
our poor Greek fleet.

One night
the sea began to rise
in waves of death,
and from Thrace
a hurricane struck.

Ship against ship,
our boats were gored
and cracked,
tossed
by the beating rain

and the violence
of the wintry storm
and the whirlwind.

Twisted and twirled
by the wicked shepherd's hand,
the ships all vanished —
disappeared!

And when the radiant dawn
arose to light the sea,
we saw the Aegean
like a garden, blooming
with dead men —
Greek men —
and the wreckage of their ships.

661   As for us and our ship,
its hull intact,
some god —
no man, however skilled,
could have done it —
laid his hand upon the helm
and brought us safely through.

Good Fortune,
wanting to save us,
boarded our ship,
so that neither on the deep,
riding on waves of death,
did we capsize,
nor driven to the rocky shore,
did we run aground.

At daybreak,
delivered from death at sea,
we could not believe our luck.

In sorrow
we thought of the fate
of our fleet,
so pitifully shaken
and wrecked by the storm.

(*a cheerful idea occurs to him*)
But wait!
If any of the others
are living still,
surely they speak of us
as we speak of them,
as men who perished,
don't you think?
And, so,
things may still turn out well.

And if any return,
you can be sure
Menelaus will be among the first.
A sunbeam
may still discover him
alive and well.
For it is not the plan of God
to wipe us out completely.
So there is hope
he'll return to us again.

You have heard all,
and you have heard the truth.
(*Waving good-bye, the* HERALD *turns and
runs through the city gates.*)

LEADER: (*slowly walking downstage, then speak-
ing*)
Helen.
Who gave you that name?
Could he foresee your destiny

681

by giving you a name of death,
O bride of spears and blood?

Helen.
Hell!
Hell on ships
and hell on men
and hell on cities.[19]

Slipping from her silken bed,
its curtains wafting
in the morning breeze,
she sailed out to sea,
running before the giant west wind.

Thousands of soldiers,
huntsmen on the track
of the oar blades'
swiftly fading footprints,
searching for those
who beached their boat
in the leafy shade of the banks
of the river Simois,[20]
came to Troy —
to struggle in blood!

699

And in Helen's name,
on a later day,
God's inexorable wrath
brought hell on Troy
for a marriage celebration —
an abomination to Zeus,
God of the Host
and God of the Guest.

At the marriage banquet,
the family of the bridegroom
raised songs to the bride

and songs to the groom
in resounding voices,
ringing with good cheer.

Now, to a different tune,
the ancient city of Priam
loudly wails,
in tears of lamentation:
"Paris took a bride
and her name was Death!"

This marriage caused his nation
to come to its end
in desolation and in tears —
needless spilling of blood.

717   NARRATOR: Once upon a time,
in his own home,
a man raised a lion cub,
taken from its mother's breast
still craving it.
At first, young and adorable,
it was the center of attention.
It played with the children
and delighted the old,
who liked to take it in their arms
like a newborn child.
And whenever it was hungry,
its eyes grew bright,
and it licked the hands
of those who would feed it.

But it grew with time,
and the lion in the blood came out.
It paid back those who nurtured it
in sheep blood —
and in death!
Horrible, ungodly feast!

The house reeked
with flowing blood,
and the family could not stop
the monstrous killer's onslaught.

This thing
they raised in their home
was ordained by God
as an instrument of doom.

737   CHORUS: So it was with Helen.

When first she came to Troy,
they called her,
on the one hand,
"high-spirited" —

but on the other hand,
"a serene sea of tranquility,"

"a precious jewel,"

"the thrill of meeting eyes,"

"new love
that fills the heart with aching."

But all that changed.

In the end,
this marriage was disastrous
to Priam's palace.
It brought Bad Luck,
who entered
and lived there
along with Priam's children.

Zeus,

God of the Host
and God of the Guest,
brought a vengeance
to make brides weep.

There is an old saying:
"Riches beget riches
and end in misery."

I disagree.
The saying should rather be:
"Evil comes from evil
endlessly."

(*The palace doors open.*
        CLYTEMNESTRA *parts the draperies and*
appears.   She crosses the porch and
stands at the head of the staircase.
        The doors close.)

An evil deed
bears ugly children,
while beautiful children
spring from Righteousness.

763   Reckless Daring,
when she grows up,
conceives —
for her pleasure! —
a darling child
from the evil deeds of men.
At the appointed time,
she gives birth
without hard labor —
easily! —
to that demon Wild Daring,
who looks just like his mother.
And when he grows up,

he comes to darken even more
the shadowy
house of Ruin.

Righteousness shines
through the thickest smoke
in the sootiest homes.
But in shrines
filled with golden treasure
acquired with filthy hands,
she looks away
and leaves.
For the sacred
is now profaned.
Righteousness does not worship before
abuse of power
or ill-gotten gains
or undeserved praise.

(*in unison*)
Righteousness brings all things
to their just conclusion.

(*In the distance a trumpet sounds from the
direction of the sea, followed by faint triumphal music. All characters freeze.*

*The palace doors open and remain so
until the end of the act.*

CLYTEMNESTRA'S ATTENDANTS *part the
draperies and step out from the palace.
They join* CLYTEMNESTRA *and position
themselves at various places upon the
porch.*

*The trumpet sounds again, followed
again by triumphal music, much closer
than before. The trumpet sounds a third
time, followed by triumphal music, just
outside the city gates, and the loud cheer-*

ing of the offstage crowds can be heard.

The LEADER *and other members of the* CHORUS *open the city gates.*

With great fanfare, foot SOLDIERS *of* AGAMEMNON *enter bearing flags and spears, along with golden urns and other plundered wealth of Troy.*

AGAMEMNON *enters driving a chariot. He is dressed in full armor, including a helmet.*

CASSANDRA *is sitting beside him, downstage so that she is clearly visible. She is motionless, her face devoid of expression, and she remains so throughout the act. She wears white robes and a necklace of flowers and holds a staff.*

The moment the chariot enters, the CHORUS *begins to cheer loudly and enthusiastically. The chariot comes to a stop center stage to increased cheering.*

The SOLDIERS *pass flags to the* CHORUS, *then position themselves around the courtyard, standing at attention with their spears upright, their shields against their chests.*

All the while, CLYTEMNESTRA *and her* ATTENDANTS *remain motionless on the palace porch, watching the proceedings.*

When the commotion begins to die down, the LEADER *advances from the periphery toward the chariot.* AGAMEMNON *removes his helmet and cradles it in his right arm. The cheering ends.*)

782   LEADER: Behold, my king!
              Conqueror of Troy!
              Beloved son of Atreus!

How best to greet you?
How do you justice? —
not too much,
not too little,
but just the right amount!

Many pretend
in front of the king.
When he has misfortune,
they look sad.
But the teeth of sorrow
come nowhere near
to biting at their hearts.
When he is glad,
they torture their faces
with false smiles.
But the shepherd
who knows his flock
by looking at their eyes
can quickly recognize
the smile of watered-down love
pretending the full-bodied heart.

As for me,
when you marshaled the army
for Helen's sake,
your image diminished
in my mind.
I shall not hide it!

You seemed out of your mind
to bring home
that self-indulgent woman
by blood
and sacrifice
and death of men.

Now,

love drawn
from deep in my heart,
I hail you!

806   Your work is accomplished.
And a job well done brings joy.

Ask around,
and you will find out
soon enough
who has been minding the house —
and who has not.

(*More cheers, louder than before. After a few moments,* AGAMEMNON *hands his helmet to one of the* SOLDIERS *and raises his arms to hush the crowd. When the crowd is quiet, he speaks with arms outspread.*)

AGAMEMNON: Argos! My Argos!

(*More cheers. After a moment,* AGAMEMNON *raises his face and arms to heaven, and the crowd grows silent.*)

O great gods of this land!
I call upon you first,
for that is only proper.
You helped me accomplish
revenge on Troy,
and you helped
bring me safely home.

(*facing the crowd*)
That nation's pleading
did not move the gods.
They cast their votes unanimously
in the ballot box of blood:[21]

"Troy must die
and all her people."
No hands came near
the other box —
only Hope.
Not one vote fell there.
(*wild cheering from the crowd*)

818   Even now,
smoke proclaims
the fall of Troy.
The clouds of her destruction
live on.
And her fat wealth
shoots up in sparks
from the dying embers.
(*more cheering from the crowd*)

For this victory
let us give thanks
and praises to the gods!
(*thunderous cheering from the crowd*)

All because of a woman,
we snared that nation
in our net of vengeance.
And the great wooden horse,
that fierce Greek beast,
trampled Troy to death!

With the setting
of the Pleiades,
the horse gave birth precipitously
to our lionhearted men.
And a man-eating lion
leaped over the towers of Troy,
appeasing its hunger
by lapping the blood of kings.

For all this
I thank the gods.

(AGAMEMNON *turns and points to the* LEAD-
ER, *who advances toward him and stops in
front of the chariot.* AGAMEMNON *speaks
to him.*)

As for your thoughts,
which I heard
and took to heart,
I agree.

It is true.
Few kinsmen and friends
have the goodness of heart
to respect
a loved one's good fortune
without begrudging him.
As for the bitter man
possessed by envy's madness,
a cold wind
blowing against his heart,
his burden only doubles.
Already overwhelmed by misery,
he winces again
at his neighbor's joy.

I am qualified to speak,
for I have seen,
and I know,
this mirror of friendship,
this shadow of a ghost,
these men who seem
sincerest friends.

841   Only one,

Ulysses —
and he did not even want to sail! —
he alone was ever loyal.
He always made himself
available to me,
as if we were yoked
and tied together.
And that is true now
whether he is alive
or dead.

Regarding other matters —
our nation,
and whether we are all
worshipping the gods
the same way[22a] —
we shall call a meeting
of the General Assembly
and take counsel.
We shall examine
to find out what is healthy
and keep it that way.
As for that which needs a cure,
we shall use —
as cheerfully as we can —
medicine, cautery, or the knife
to remove the corruption.[22b]

(*turning toward the palace and facing*
CLYTEMNESTRA, *but not addressing her or*
acknowledging her presence)
Oh, royal palace and home!
(*to heaven*)
O gods who sent me forth
and brought me safely back!
Let my present victory last!

(*The crowd shouts and cheers even more*

*thunderously and enthusiastically than
before.* AGAMEMNON *smiles and waves to
them and makes no attempt to stop the
cheering.*

After a while, CLYTEMNESTRA *begins to
speak, but the cheering of the crowd
drowns her out. She tries again, somewhat louder, still without success. Finally,
in a booming voice, she catches their attention, and they begin to grow silent.*

AGAMEMNON, *by raising his arm, quiets
the crowd.*

All heads but that of CASSANDRA *turn
to* CLYTEMNESTRA .   *There is absolute silence. In a normal voice she begins her
speech anew.*)

855   CLYTEMNESTRA : People of Argos,
            gathered here,
            I am not ashamed
            to speak aloud
            before all of you
            of the love I bear my husband.
            In the course of time
            modesty fades.
            That is only human.

            What I tell now
            I tell firsthand,
            the sad story of my life
            all the years
            my husband was away at Troy.

            It is a bad and terrible thing
            for a wife to sit around the house
            all by herself,
            no man around,
            hearing rumors

that, like a fever, vanish,
only to return again.

A messenger comes with fearful news.
Quick on his heels comes another,
crying out to the whole household
worse news still.

Had Agamemnon
sustained all the wounds
in stories told to me,
he would have been
as full of holes
as any fishing net.
Had he died
as often
as rumor said he did,
he would have been
a triple-bodied monster
returning from the dead.
For he died
at least three times!

Because such tales
disturbed my peace of mind,
several times
they had to cut me down
from the rope with which
I hanged myself.

(*The members of the* CHORUS *look at one
another in disbelief.*)

That is why
our son Orestes,
in whom our love is pledged
and sealed,
is not here with us today

where he belongs.

(AGAMEMNON *looks concerned.*)

No cause for alarm!
881 He is with Strophius of Phocis,
your faithful friend,
who spoke to me of peril
on two accounts —
of your danger at Troy
and of the danger
of revolution
here at home.

The people were clamoring,
and there was danger
of their overthrowing
the government.
(*low grumblings among the* CHORUS *members*)

It is human nature
to trample on the underdog.
(*louder grumblings*)

That is my excuse —
as you can see —
completely free
of guile.

As for me,
the wellsprings of my tears
have all gone dry.
Not one drop left.
My eyes still ache
from all my weeping.

Late at night,

when I feared that
woodpiles for beacons
set up so long ago for you
had been abandoned
forever,
when a mosquito's
whispering and buzzing
disturbed my sleep,
I saw you suffer
more wounds
than ever possible
in that short sleeping time.

Now all suffering is over
and done with.
Free of grief,
I greet my husband.

(CLYTEMNESTRA *descends the staircase and
walks toward the chariot. Halfway there,
facing* AGAMEMNON, *she falls to her knees
and assumes a position of abject obei-
sance, with elbows, forearms, and hands
flat against the ground, converging toward* AGAMEMNON, *her head bowed.*

The CHORUS *reacts in revulsion because groveling was uncharacteristic of
the Greeks, who considered it the behavior
of barbarians.*

AGAMEMNON *watches in astonishment.*

After a moment, still kneeling,
CLYTEMNESTRA *raises her upper body and
head erect, spreading her arms as if to
embrace* AGAMEMNON, *and speaks in a
loud, clear voice. She proceeds to deliver
a list of items of great value, comparing*
AGAMEMNON *to each of them, and she
pauses after each item so that he may*

savor them all.)

Watchdog of our flock and home!

Stay that keeps the mast erect!

Post that holds the towering roof!

A father's only son!²³

Land when sailors' hope is gone!

Splendor of daybreak
after a night of storm!

Sparkling water
the thirsty traveler strays upon!

(CLYTEMNESTRA *slowly rises; when stand-*
ing, she resumes her speech to AGAMEM-
NON, *who is entranced by her words.*)

Oh, it is sweet
to be free
from all responsibility!

(*to the* CHORUS)
This is my greeting to him,
and how well he deserves it!
Let no one bear me malice
for any harm I may have caused.
My burden was great.
(*walking downstage and around to the*
rear — the open side — of the chariot)

906   Now, dearest,
step down from the chariot,
but do not let your foot,

my lord, conqueror of Troy,
touch the earth!

Slave-women!
Why this delay?
You know what you should do!
Lay the draperies[24]
upon the ground
before his feet.
Let him walk a crimson[25a] path
into the home
he never expected to see,
but where Justice
has led him.

(CLYTEMNESTRA'S ATTENDANTS *carefully remove all the draperies from the doorway and from the walls of the hall. They perform an ominous dance before and while they lay them, with hesitancy, on the ground, from the foot of the staircase all the way to the open rear end of the chariot. On the ground, the draperies form a highly visible arc downstage of the chariot.*

When all the draperies have been laid, the ATTENDANTS *return to the porch to watch the proceedings in horror along with the rest of the crowd, which believes it is a sacrilege to lay beautiful treasure on the ground.*

AGAMEMNON, *maintaining his regal posture, is more puzzled than horrified.*)

CLYTEMNESTRA : (*continuing aside*)
Regarding other matters,
patience will at last be rewarded.
And with the help of the gods,

the just plan of Fate
shall be executed.

AGAMEMNON: (*to* CLYTEMNESTRA, *who turns to face
him*)
Daughter of Leda,
you who kept my house for me,
in a way
your welcome matches my absence.
It was strained to great length!
But it is for others, not you,
to praise me so!

918

Furthermore,
do not — as if I were a woman —
make me out so precious
or — as if I were a barbarian king —
shout out so loud
and grovel in the dust for me.

And do not build a road
that leads to hatred
by spreading
many-colored[25b] splendors
upon the ground.

That is for gods.
The very thought
of a man
trampling on treasure
makes me tremble.

I am a man, not a god.
Treat me accordingly.
Different, too,
is a doormat from a drapery.

Good judgment

is God's most precious gift to man.
Wealthy is he
who lives out his days
abounding in this gift.

And if I exercise it now
and for the rest of my days,
and do not give in
to your unreasonable demands,
then I will deserve
to be called a man of courage.

CLYTEMNESTRA : (*walking up to* AGAMEMNON, *intimately*)
Don't defy me!
Trust me!
My advice is good!

AGAMEMNON: (*intimately*)
No! My mind is made up.
I shall not change it for you.

CLYTEMNESTRA : You fear the gods!

AGAMEMNON: I know what I am doing.
No man ever knew it better.
It is final!

CLYTEMNESTRA : Had Priam been victorious,
what would he have done?

AGAMEMNON: I well believe
he might have walked on draperies!

CLYTEMNESTRA : You fear what men might say!

AGAMEMNON: The voice of the people
is a mighty force.

CLYTEMNESTRA : They always envy
            the man of good fortune.

940   AGAMEMNON: What is the matter with you?
            Is this womanly,
            this desire for conflict?

CLYTEMNESTRA : It is fitting
            even for victorious kings
            to lose now and then.

AGAMEMNON: Why does winning
            this argument
            mean so much to you?

CLYTEMNESTRA : Let me win this time!
            You can!
            Do it of your own free will!

AGAMEMNON: (*publicly*)
            Very well, then!
            Here, someone!
            Take off my sandals,
            the slaves to my feet.
            And as I crush
            these purple[25c] splendors
            so richly colored by the sea,
            may God not take revenge on me.

            What extravagance!
            I am ashamed
            to plunder my own house
            by trampling on its treasure.
            Enough!

            (*One of* CLYTEMNESTRA'S ATTENDANTS *removes his sandals. As she does,* AGAMEM-

NON *smiles at her.   Then the smile fades,
and he looks at* CLYTEMNESTRA *and speaks
to her as he gently places a hand on* CAS-
SANDRA*'s shoulder.*)

Take this stranger-girl inside
and be kind.
The eyes of God
gaze fondly
on the victor who is gentle.
No one wants to be a slave.

(*gazing lovingly at* CASSANDRA; *slowly,
softly, tenderly, controlling his desire except for the stroking of* CASSANDRA*'s hair*)
She is a gift from my army,
of all my possessions
the loveliest.

(*with yearning and tenderness*)
She has come here
(*breathing audibly*)
with me.

(*abruptly awakening from his enchant-
ment; to* CLYTEMNESTRA)
Now, since you've talked me into it,
I shall crush purple underfoot
as I go into my palace.

(CLYTEMNESTRA, *never stepping upon the
draperies and always somewhat downstage of them, extends a hand to* AGAMEM-
NON, *who takes it after a moment's hesitation and slowly descends from the chariot.
    Once both his feet are upon the
draperies,* AGAMEMNON *stops in his tracks,
almost as if held there by an invisible*

*force. Suddenly he is terrified. He looks
down at his feet, then slowly turns his face
toward heaven, then looks down at his feet
again. This time when he raises his head,
he looks at the members of the* CHORUS, *all
of whom have an expression of horror, as
do his* SOLDIERS *and* CLYTEMNESTRA'S AT-
TENDANTS.

CASSANDRA *remains seated in the chariot, motionless and devoid of expression,
seemingly oblivious to the proceedings.*

CLYTEMNESTRA *is not horrified; on the
contrary, she is smiling. Facing* AGAMEM-
NON *and slightly downstage of the
draperies, she takes a few steps back from*
AGAMEMNON *in the direction of the palace,
all the while encouraging and beckoning
him with her hands. She walks backward
and parallel to but not touching the
draperies. When she has reached downstage center, she stops, stands erect, and
speaks to* AGAMEMNON, *who is still standing frozen at the rear of the chariot.*)

958   CLYTEMNESTRA : (*standing still, upright and firm,
pointing to the sea*)
The sea is over there,
and who can drain it dry?
It breeds an endless supply
of the purple,
precious as silver,
with which we dye our fabrics.
And by God's grace,
this House
has more than its share.
Poverty is a thing
beyond its comprehension.

And yet,
I would have trampled on
every single splendid thing —
had the oracles so demanded —
to bring you safely home.

(CLYTEMNESTRA *smiles comfortingly at*
AGAMEMNON, *and then she resumes her*
backward march to the palace steps, all
the while beckoning AGAMEMNON *with her*
hands. When she reaches the foot of the
staircase, she stops. She holds out both
arms to AGAMEMNON *like a mother encour-*
aging a child to take its first step.

AGAMEMNON *still has not moved from*
his position at the rear of the chariot. He
tests his feet and discovers they are not
paralyzed. Delighted that he has not been
struck down by the gods, he begins to
walk in the direction of the palace.

AGAMEMNON*'s walk is in fact a dance*
in slow motion, with rhythmic paces dur-
ing which he looks at the crowd and raises
his arms from time to time as public fig-
ures do. As he proceeds, he grows ever
more confident that he deserves this ex-
traordinary treatment and furthermore
that the gods approve of it. He smiles
broadly, radiantly, and triumphantly,
waving from time to time to the horrified
crowd, whose horror he can no longer
see. Neither can he hear the deathly si-
lence.

As he advances toward the staircase,
to show his bravado, he begins to trample
the draperies in a variety of ways, occa-
sionally stomping, goose-stepping, and
even scraping them like a horse or a dog

pawing the earth. When he arrives at the foot of the staircase, he stops.

    CLYTEMNESTRA *takes his hands in hers.* CLYTEMNESTRA *and* AGAMEMNON *face each other, he on the draperies, she on the bare ground next to them. She gently strokes his neck and cheeks. Then she resumes her speech.*)

As long as the root lives,
leaves come again
to shade the house
against the Dog Star's heat.

And now you have returned
to your palace, your home.

You are a sign
of a mild winter.

And when Zeus makes
the green clustered grapes
ripe for wine,
it will be cool in the house.

For the master is home.

(CLYTEMNESTRA *kisses* AGAMEMNON *on both cheeks.*

    AGAMEMNON *turns to face the staircase but does not ascend, remaining frozen for a moment.*

    CLYTEMNESTRA *turns to face the court-yard; arms outstretched, she turns to heaven.*)

O Zeus!
Zeus Accomplisher!

Accomplish these, my prayers!
Accomplish this, Your will!

(CLYTEMNESTRA *turns to face the palace.*
She links her right arm in AGAMEMNON*'s*
left, and then together they slowly and
majestically   ascend   the   staircase.
CLYTEMNESTRA *and* AGAMEMNON *enter the*
palace.
    The doors slowly close.
    The CHORUS *and the* ATTENDANTS *look*
on anxiously. The SOLDIERS *remain at at-*
tention.
    Darkness descends.)

INTERMISSION

ACT THREE

*It is slightly later the same day. When the lights come up,
the scene is the same as it was at the end of Act Two with
the following exceptions: the* SOLDIERS, CLYTEMNESTRA'S
ATTENDANTS, *the flags, the Trojan booty, etc., are no
longer present. Neither are the draperies.* CASSANDRA *remains in the chariot, motionless. The* CHORUS *stands facing the audience in a close-knit arc before the palace.
The* LEADER *and the* PROPHET *are in the center of the arc.
The* LEADER *steps forward.*

975   LEADER: Why does Fear
               beat its wings
               so relentlessly
               against the walls
               around my heart?

      PROPHET: (*stepping forward, standing next to the*
               LEADER)
               I do not want this prophecy.
               And yet it comes,
               unrequested
               and free of charge.

               And the courage
               that dwells within my spirit
               cannot dismiss it
               like a bad dream,
               difficult to understand.

LEADER: (*taking the* PROPHET *around the shoulders, reassuringly*)
Have not time and sand
cast upon the shore
the moorings of that day
when, in ships against Ilium,
the army went to sea?
And haven't we seen
Agamemnon home again
with our very eyes?

PROPHET: Still, I hear that inner chant,
that discordant dirge
composed and sung
by the Furies
without sweet accompaniment
of harp or lyre,
(*chanting*)
"All hope is gone."

Stomach churning,
heart wildly beating,
brain whirling —
my vital organs
all gone mad
from learning things
soon to be accomplished
in the name of Justice.

And yet,
I cannot stop praying
that all the things I dread
may never come to pass.

1001   CHORUS: Good health
cannot insure its house from falling.
Sickness,

its next-door neighbor,
is always pressing hard
to break down
the common wall
that stands between.

And however careful his course,
a man will still strike
disaster's unseen and sudden reef.
If, before such time,
he receives warning,
and realizing that his ship is overloaded,
he tosses precious cargo overboard,
then at least the ship
will not go down in ruin
to the bottom of the sea.

Great and abundant the gifts of Zeus!
Year after year
He makes the bountiful spring
follow the winter's starvation.

1019   But
once the dark and mortal blood of man
has fallen to the ground,
who then can conjure spells
to call it back again?

And remember Zeus' warning:
He killed that man
who really could raise the dead![26]

Because Fate may clash with Fate,[27]
the things I fear
may never come to pass.

PROPHET : And yet
my heart,

so much swifter than my tongue,
speaks to me
at this very moment.
Deep in the dark,
where flames lick at my heart,
it grieves and howls:
"Hope, once alive,
comes to an end."

(*The palace doors open.   There are no
draperies.*   CLYTEMNESTRA   *steps forth,
crosses the porch, and stands at the head
of the staircase.   The doors remain open
during* CLYTEMNESTRA *'s entire transaction
with* CASSANDRA *.*)

1035   CLYTEMNESTRA : Cassandra,
you may go in now.

Zeus, without wrath,
has delivered you here
and requires your purification
with all the other slaves
by the washing of hands
at the altar of our household god.

(CLYTEMNESTRA *turns, intending to reenter
the palace.   After taking a few steps, she
glances back and notices that* CASSANDRA
*has not moved.   Retracing her steps, she
descends the staircase halfway.*)

Step down, then,
from the chariot.
Do not be proud.
Remember,
they say that long ago
even Hercules

was sold into bondage
and ate the bread of slaves.

Since your fate is similar,
at least be thankful
for masters
who have been rich
for generations.
Those finding themselves
with new wealth
beyond their wildest dreams
are brutal to their slaves.
Here you shall have
all you have the right to have.

LEADER: (*kindly, to* CASSANDRA)
She is speaking to you
and her words are perfectly plain.
Caught in this fateful net
in which you find yourself,
you should obey her
if you can.
Perhaps you cannot.

CLYTEMNESTRA: (*walking to the chariot, glowering
at* CASSANDRA *but speaking to the* LEADER)
I am making myself clear,
and she must obey
unless her language is gibberish
or wild as the swallow's song!

LEADER: (*to* CASSANDRA) Go with her.
What she bids is best
under the circumstances.
Obey! Step down
from the chariot!

CLYTEMNESTRA: (*to the* CHORUS)

I have no more time
to waste upon this woman.

Indoors, at the central hearth,
flocks of sheep are already standing,
waiting to be sacrificed
to commemorate this happy day
we never hoped to see.

(*angrily, looking directly at* CASSANDRA
and pointing stiff-armed at her)
You!
If you mean
to participate in the ceremonies,
be quick!

(*exasperated, slowly dropping her arm to
her side, contemptuously*)
If you do not understand,
or cannot speak my language,
then at least
make a gesture[28]
with your (*contemptuously*) *foreign* hand!

1062   LEADER: This strange girl
needs an interpreter.
She is like an animal newly trapped.

CLYTEMNESTRA :   (*turning from* CASSANDRA *and
speaking coldly as she walks toward the
palace*)
No.
It is the nation she left behind
that is newly trapped.
She is mad and entranced
by her own wild thoughts.
She is not trained for slavery,
and she will not understand

until all the rage and strength
in her blood
have been drained away.

I have no more time
for her contempt.
(CLYTEMNESTRA *ascends the staircase and
enters the palace. The doors close.*)

LEADER: I'm not angry with this child.
          I pity her.

          (*to* CASSANDRA)
          Come down, poor creature!
          Leave the chariot!
          Give in!
          Accept your fate!

          (CASSANDRA *remains motionless except for
          her head, which moves almost impercepti-
          bly.   After a few moments she slowly
          stands. Her upright body motionless, she
          turns her head to face each member of the*
          CHORUS *and finally the* LEADER.
          The LEADER *extends his hand.   She
          slowly takes it and slowly descends. Once
          on the ground,* CASSANDRA *turns her head
          this way and that. Then she does a bizar-
          re, animalistic dance.*
          *While she is dancing, the chariot is
          slowly and inconspicuously pushed off-
          stage through the city gates, which close
          after it. She does not begin to speak until
          the chariot has disappeared and her
          dance is completed.*)

CASSANDRA : (*uttering a wail of despair, her face
          without expression*)

Oh-OH-oh,   O Oh-OH-oh! (*an inarticu-
late expression with the meter of the following line:*)
Apollo, O Apollo!

LEADER: Why Apollo in your distress?
Of all the gods in heaven,
he understands misfortune least.

CASSANDRA: (*as before*)
Oh-OH-oh, O Oh-OH-oh!
Apollo, O Apollo!

1078   CHORUS: Again she calls upon that god
who wants nothing to do
with lamentation.

CASSANDRA: (*wailing in despair*)
Apollo, O Apollo!
Lord who has destroyed me!
You have done it again —
completely!

CHORUS: I think she means to prophesy
her own doom.
Even in her slave's heart
the divine gift lives on.

CASSANDRA: (*as before*)
Apollo, O Apollo!
God of the Highways!
Lord who has ruined me!
Down which highway
have you led me this time?
Whose house is this?

LEADER: The House of Atreus
and his sons.

Do you understand?

CASSANDRA : (*flatly*)
    No, this is a house that hates God,
    a house guilty of family bloodshed
    and torture —
    a slaughterhouse
    with a bloodstained floor.

CHORUS : (*amazed*)
    O stranger
    keen-scented,
    like a bloodhound
    hot upon the trail!

CASSANDRA : (*suddenly pointing in terror above
    the heads of the audience*)
    Look! My witnesses!
    Little children
    crying
    over their own butchery and death
    and their own brown-roasted flesh
    their father feasted on.

CHORUS : We've heard of your prophetic skill!

    It is famous!

    But we don't need it
    at the moment!

    We have enough prophets here!

1100   CASSANDRA : (*frightened*)
    O my gods!
    What is she up to?
    What monstrous horror
    does she plan

> within the palace walls?
> To kill the husband
> she does not love?
> And help is far away.

CHORUS: I can make nothing
> of this prophecy.

> The others I understood,
> for the whole city echoes
> with talk of them.

CASSANDRA :   (*frightened and pantomiming*)
> You are so vicious, then,
> you can do this?
> Your husband —
> the man who shares your bed —
> is delighting in his bath.
> Is this the way it's going to end?
> Done with dispatch!
> One hand gropes,
> now the other.

CHORUS: I am lost
> in the darkness of her speech.

> I do not understand.

CASSANDRA :   (*terrified*)
> Look! Look!
> What is that?
> A net of death?

> Or is the snare
> the woman there?
> She, once partner in his bed,
> now partner in his murder.[29]

(*emotionless*)
O Vengeance!
Are you never satisfied?
How you howl this accursed death
for all to hear!

1119   CHORUS: What sort of vengeance
                 are you talking about
                 that shouts so loud
                 throughout this House?

                 You take all hope away.

                 I feel as if
                 I'm wounded in my heart,
                 and the blood is pouring out,
                 and the light is growing dim
                 as death is setting in.

CASSANDRA: (*frightened, rapidly*)
                 Ah! Ah!
                 See there! See there!
                 The black-horned cow
                 is charging her bull!
                 Is there no one to stop her?
                 He is caught in a net
                 in a tank of water!
                 Now she is goring him!
                 He is going down, down.

                 (*without emotion, slowly*)
                 I am talking to you of treachery
                 and of a murder in a bath.

CHORUS: I am no expert
                 when it comes to prophecy,
                 but even I
                 can see the horror in this.

What good is prophecy?
Such skill in words is evil,
terrifying those
who learn the future.[30]

CASSANDRA : (*sitting down, embracing her knees,
            rocking and wailing*)
          Oh, oh, my ill-starred life.
          Misery floods upon me.
          Why have you brought me here,
          miserable creature that I am?
          Why? Why?
          Except to die with him.
          What else?

1140 CHORUS: You are mad
          and sick at heart
          to sing your own death song,
          like the brown nightingale
          singing her wild lyric —
          "Itys, Itys!" —
          over and over again,
          weeping forever and grieving,
          a life full of tears.

CASSANDRA : (*with yearning*)
          Oh, for the nightingale's song
          and a fate like hers![31]
          The gods gave her wings to fly —
          sweet life without sorrow.

          (*despairingly*)
          I keep expecting
          to be cleaved in two
          by a double-edged blade.

CHORUS: Where are you going

in this torrent of tears,
inspired yet insane?

Why do you chant
songs of terror
in wailing cries
that reach the skies?

Is there no end
to this voyage of prophecy,
given by God
but filled with evil?

CASSANDRA : (*kneeling, despairingly*)
       Marriage of Paris —
       death to those dearest to me!

       (*nostalgically*)
       Oh, Scamander[32] —
       whose waters my family used to drink!
       Time was, I, too,
       refreshed at your springs.
       (*pantomiming drinking from the river with
       great pleasure*)

       (*despairingly*)
       Ah, me!
1160   Now I cry
       my prophecy
       by the rivers of death,
       on the banks of Cocytus
       and sad Acheron.[33]

CHORUS: You speak so clearly
       a newborn child could understand.

       Like a dagger dealing death,
       your high-pitched song of agony,

born of your cruel fate,
makes my blood freeze.

CASSANDRA : (*slowly standing, then speaking despairingly*)
Oh, the sorrow, the sorrow
of my annihilated city!
The sacrifices
my father made at her wall,
the flocks of sheep
slaughtered there —
no use at all
to save our nation
from destruction.

(*without emotion*)
I, too,
yes, I,
my feverish brain ablaze,
shall die.

CHORUS : And so you chant
the same old song!

Is there an evil spirit here
crushing you,
making you cry
this song of death
and pain past endurance?

Is there no end?

1178   CASSANDRA : (*authoritatively, rapidly but clearly*)
No longer
shall my prophecy glance
like some young bride
from under her wedding veil.
Rather, it shall burst forth

as strong as winds that blow at dawn,
bright as the sun rising over the swell,
shining at last upon these woes.

Now I shall speak plainly,
and not in riddles.

Bear witness
as I run at their heels,
hot on the scent
of brutal things
done long ago.

(*normal tempo*)
Within this House
a choir sings
from dawn to dusk
and on to dawn again.
They drink and grow rowdy,
these revelers in this House,
and they will not go away —
their melody discordant,
their lyric far from gay.

Who are these carousers?
The Furies —
the Sisters of Vengeance!
They are drunk on human blood!
They hang around the halls
and raise a rousing chorus
of the first crime in this House.

(*slowly*)
Then, one by one, they vomit.

(*normal tempo*)
The song they sing goes like this:
(*singing*)

"A brother loved his brother's wife.[34]
Well traveled o'er, this road to strife."

Did I go wide of the mark
or hit it like a master bowman?

Am I some false prophet
hawking lies from door to door?

I take an oath —
bear witness! —
I know by heart and well
the story of the ancient evil
carried by this House.

1198   CHORUS: What good are oaths?

And yet we are amazed!

Reared in an alien city
far beyond the sea,
you strike the truth
as if you'd seen it yourself!

CASSANDRA : (*coquettishly, boastfully*)
Apollo taught me my craft.

CHORUS: Apollo *loved you*, then?

CASSANDRA : Time was
I blushed to speak of it.

CHORUS: (*sarcastically*)
I'm not surprised.
When you were a princess,
you could afford
to put on airs.

CASSANDRA : (*defensively*)
    He wanted me
    and tried to take me.
    He told me that he loved me.

CHORUS: (*in amazement, incredulously*)
    You made love, then,
    with Apollo?

CASSANDRA : (*hesitantly, somberly*)
    I promised.
    But I broke my word.

CHORUS: Ah! But before!
    Had he already given you
    the gift of prophecy?

CASSANDRA : Yes.
    Already I foresaw
    all my nation's suffering.

CHORUS: Apollo did not punish you
    out of spite?
    How can that be?

CASSANDRA : Oh, he did!
    Afterward,
    I could still prophesy,
    but no one — no one! —
    believed me!

LEADER: All you foretell
    seems true enough to me.

CASSANDRA : (*crying out in pain*)
    Oo, oo, oh, oh, the pain!
    I cannot concentrate!
    My mind is whirling and hurling

toward new and terrible prophecy!

(*suddenly pointing above the palace, her
pain abruptly ending but the horror continuing*)
Look, there!
Hovering over the House,
shadows of dreams,
so small and young —
children! —
darlings
killed by those they loved.

They hold up their bowels,
their hearts, and their livers,
which their own father ate.
Horrible!

(*authoritatively*)
I tell you,
someone plots revenge for this.

The lion, too cowardly to hunt,
rolled in the master's bed
and had the run of the house
until the master returned —
(*realizing her own predicament*)
my master, too,
now that I'm a slave.

(*with despair and anger*)
Captain of ships,
king who tore Ilium
out by the roots,
what does he know
of the hateful bitch
who licks his cheek
and wags her tail

and then,
like Vengeance himself,
executes him!

(*authoritatively*)
When the female
cuts down the male,
that is true Daring.

(*hatefully*)
By what name should I call her
to do her justice?
What poison beast?
Viper,
striking from any direction?
Scylla,
monster lurking in rocks,
harmful to sailors
that roam the sea?
Dragon-mother-from-hell,
snorting fire
of unforgiving revenge
onto her own family?

How she cried out triumphantly,
so loudly all could hear,
pretending joy for his safe return
from the war and from the sea —
as if announcing victory!

(*with resignation*)
What does it matter
if people believe me or not?

What will be will be.
And soon you will see
my words were true.

1242   CHORUS: I understood Thyestes' feast
            upon his children's flesh,
            and I was terrified,
            for you told the truth,
            not tales.
            I heard the rest
            but missed its meaning.

CASSANDRA : (*slowly and emphatically*)
            Now you shall understand:
            Agamemnon dies this day!

LEADER: My poor child!
            Tell happy things!

CASSANDRA : Useless.
            This story has no God of Healing.

LEADER: What must be must be.
            Yet I pray what you say
            may never come to pass.

CASSANDRA : Prayers. Of course.
            But *they* do not pray.
            They plan to strike!

LEADER: What man is doing
            this monstrous thing?

CASSANDRA : What *man*?
            You do not understand.

LEADER: Perhaps.
            I could not follow everything.

CASSANDRA : But I speak good Greek —
            too good, I think.

LEADER: And Apollo's oracle
at Delphi
also speaks Greek,
but she is hard to understand.

CASSANDRA: (*crying out in pain, then sitting and
rocking, lying on one side then the other,
embracing her knees*)
1256
Aiee, aiee! Oh, such fire!
Apollo, my Lord, King of Light!
You are consuming me!
Aiee! Oh-OH-oh-OH!

(*Her pain ends abruptly.   She slowly
stands, then speaks without emotion.*)
The lioness who sleeps with the wolf
while her proud lion ranges far away
shall slay me, poor wretch that I am.
She is preparing a drug,
my reward for coming here.

And now she is sharpening a blade
to kill her husband,
his reward for bringing me here.

(*shouting*)
Vengeance scores a victory!

(*angrily*)
Why do I carry this mockery,
this staff of prophecy?
(*hurling her staff down upon the ground*)

Why wear this necklace of flowers?
At least I will ruin you before I die!
(*She pulls off her floral necklace, crushes
the flowers one by one in her hands, and
lets them fall to the ground.*)

Down with you!
This, for all you've done to me!
Let someone else
be rich in doom!

(*After the last crushed flower has fallen,
she remains standing erect, suddenly
caught in a trance. Almost magically, her
prophetic robes slip off her body, as if removed by an invisible force, and fall to
the ground. Whether she is left standing
nude or wearing a slip-like white under-
garment is at the discretion of the director.
She continues in a matter-of-fact way.*)

Behold!
Apollo has stripped me
of my prophetic robes!

(*A member of the* CHORUS *with a cloak immediately removes it from himself and covers her with it.   She examines her new
clothing with curiosity and resumes speaking.*)

Even while I was still wearing
ordinary clothing,
(*fingering the cloak*)
Apollo used to punish me
by having all those dearest to me
become my enemies
and perpetually curse and mock me.

They were so wrong.

How they used to make fun of me:
"Look at the crazy girl!"

or
"Look at the charlatan!"
or
"Look how she crouches
like a poor, starving wretch!"

I endured it all.

And now
Apollo is through with me,
his oracle.
That's why he's led me
to this house of death.

My father's altars
are destroyed.
In their place
stands a chopping block
to butcher a victim
and spill hot blood —
my own.

1279   The two of us will die,
but not unavenged![35]

Orestes shall return home
to slay his mother —
a death for his father's blood.
An exile, wanderer of the earth,
banished from house and home,
he shall return
and make an end to the evil upon evil
within his family.[36]

This oath was sworn
by the great gods on high:
"His father's corpse
shall summon him home."

(*Her mood abruptly changes.   Serenity
descends upon her, and for a moment she
is almost happy.*)
Then, why weep?
After all,
I who saw Troy destroyed
now see her destroyers
doomed by the gods.

(*pointing to the palace doors*)
Those doors
are the gates to the underworld.
Soon I shall pass through them
and meet my fate.
I accept my death.

(*dropping her arm and turning toward the*
CHORUS)
I only pray
the stroke is true,
that I do not struggle,
and with a rush of blood,
without pain,
I close my eyes
and die.

LEADER: My poor child,
       you have suffered much,
       and you are wise beyond your years.
       That is clear from all you say.
       Yet, if you know it to be true,
       this death that is upon you,
       how can you walk to God's altar
       serene as an ox for sacrifice?

CASSANDRA: There is no escape.

1300 LEADER : There still is time.

CASSANDRA : My time has come.
        I cannot win by flight.

LEADER : Cassandra, you are brave.
        You endure much.

CASSANDRA : Only the sorrowful
        ever hear such praise.

LEADER : Blessed are they
        that nobly die.

CASSANDRA : (*sympathetically to the* LEADER *as she
        prophesies the death of his own sons with-
        out his comprehension*)
        Woe unto you, my father,
        for your noble sons.
        (*starting in terror*)

LEADER : What is it?
        What horrifies you so?

CASSANDRA : (*crying out in pain*)
        Oh! Oh!

LEADER : There's nothing here
        to cause you pain —
        unless some horror
        in your mind.

CASSANDRA : (*frightened and cowering*)
        The room within reeks with blood.
        It is like a slaughterhouse.

LEADER : (*reassuringly*)
        Only sacrificial animals

butchered at the hearth.

CASSANDRA : It has the odor
of an open grave.

LEADER: Only incense from Arabia.

CASSANDRA :   (*in resignation, with a touch of
warmth*)
I am going in.
And as I go,
I mourn my own death
and Agamemnon's.
My life is over.

Dear friends, really,
I am not a bird
shrieking in vain
over horrors done
in a bush!37

Remember the manner of my death
when a woman is killed
in payment for me,
and a man is killed
in payment for
that miserably mated man.38

I ask this of you
as a stranger about to die.

1321   LEADER: Poor suffering creature,
I pity you
and the fate you see so clear.

CASSANDRA : These are the last words
I shall ever speak:
No more shall I lament for me,

no more sing of my own death.

(*prayerfully, with arms outstretched*)
O Sun!
O last rays of shining light!
Make my killers pay
for a gentle slave-girl,
brutally murdered.

(*smiling ironically*)
What a joke — the human condition!
Good Fortune
can be changed
by a shadow,
(*solemnly*)
and one swipe
of a wet sponge
can wipe out a picture.
And that,
of all things human,
is most pitiful of all.

(CASSANDRA, *the eyes of the* CHORUS *upon her, slowly and regally ascends the palace steps. Even though the doors are still shut, she continues to walk across the porch without any hesitation, as if she knows they will open for her.*

The palace doors open.

Without breaking her stride, CASSANDRA *enters.*

The doors close behind her.

After a moment, the LEADER *turns from the palace doors to the rest of the* CHORUS. *As he begins to speak, the members of the* CHORUS *slowly turn, one by one, from the palace doors, where their eyes have been glued, to face the* LEADER.)

LEADER: Rich men
are never rich enough.
None of them
has ever pointed
a finger to the door
and said in words
loud and clear
to even more riches,
"Go away!
My doors
are forever locked to you.
Do not come again!"

CHORUS: The gods gave
Priam's nation to our king.
They honored him
with safe return.
Must Agamemnon now bleed
for bygone generations,
die for those already slain,
and by dying
cause more death to come?

(*in unison*)
Is there a man alive
born free of this fiendish curse?

AGAMEMNON: (*shouting in surprise, terror, and
agony from within the palace*)
O gods!
I am being stabbed to death!

1343

LEADER: (*startled and frightened*)
Hush! Who can that be
who cries of his own murder?

AGAMEMNON: (*as before*)

My gods!
Again!
Wounded twice!

LEADER: It is the king!
It's done, the thing!
Let every man
suggest a plan.[39]

CHORUS: Here's what I suggest:
Get help! That's always best!

LEADER: Better act at once!
Catch them both,
their blade in blood!

CHORUS: (*in unison, all pointing to the* LEADER)
Agreed! You lead!

Who cannot see
that these steps they have taken
lead but to tyranny
here in the nation?

But we are wasting time!
We chat, say this and that,
while they commit the crime!

I'm not sure
just what we should do.
But I think
even men of action
should first make a plan.

1360   Yes, I agree!
But I fail to see
how by words
we can set dead men

back on their feet!

Do you suggest
we give in to their power —
live out our days in tyranny's tower?

(*in unison*)
We can never do that.
Death is sweeter by far —
by far —
than a life under tyranny!

How can we be sure,
just because we heard a cry,
that the king is dead?

We should know the truth,
know the facts,
give up idle speculation,
before venting wrath!

LEADER: (*ascending the staircase halfway, then
             turning to face the* CHORUS)
             You force me to decide.
             Well then, first and foremost,
             we must know
             how it goes
             with Agamemnon.

(*The palace doors fly open.*
      CLYTEMNESTRA, *hands covered with
blood, stands over the bloody corpses of*
AGAMEMNON *and* CASSANDRA.
      AGAMEMNON *is lying slumped in a sil-
ver bathtub, his body covered with and
tangled in one of the purple and crimson
draperies he recently walked upon.* CAS-
SANDRA *lies on the floor next to him.*

[*A Greek theater would require the ec-cyclema to slowly carry forward* CASSAN-DRA*'s and* AGAMEMNON*'s corpses. Alter-natively, mirrors could achieve the same effect.*]
    The LEADER *staggers backward down the staircase while the* CHORUS *screams in horror.*)

CLYTEMNESTRA :   (*matter-of-factly*)
        Before,
        I said many things —
        out of necessity.
        Now, unashamed,
        I unsay them all.

        How else could I,
        filled with such hate
        against such a *loving* husband,
        catch him in my net of no escape,
        without pretending tenderness?

        You see,
        with time,
        this act of mine,
        so long remembering a crime
        committed in other days,
        has finally come to pass.

        (*pausing after each sentence for emphasis*)
        This is where I killed him.
        It is done.
        I did it.
        And I do not deny it.
        (*removing the drapery over* AGAMEMNON*'s corpse*)

1381   As fishermen cast huge, encircling nets,

I cast this —
(*casting the drapery over the corpse like a*
fisherman casting a net)
my most treasured drapery —
that he might not escape
and prevent his death.

I caught him fast.
Then I stabbed him twice (*pantomiming*).
With two great cries
his thighs went limp.
And when he was dead,
I dealt him a third blow —
just for good measure —
and in thanksgiving and reverence
to the God of the Underworld.

As he lay dying,
and the life was struggling out of him,
I was drenched
in the short, quick spurts
of the dark red rain
of bloody sacrifice.

And I rejoiced,
as cheerful as sown fields in spring
beneath heaven-sent showers,
as the earth gives birth
to green shoots.

These are the facts,
old people of Argos.
Rejoice —
if you would rejoice.
As for me,
I am exultant!

If there were such a thing

as a wine of curses to pour over the slain,
this man would deserve —
more than deserve —
such a sacrament.
He filled our cup
with accursedly evil things.
Now he has come home
and has himself
drunk it
to the dregs.

1399   CHORUS: We are stunned.
How can you speak like this —
so arrogantly —
above our fallen king?

(SOLDIERS *carrying spears and armed with swords appear from all directions and surround the palace staircase. One* SOLDIER *slowly ascends the staircase to identify the dead man. He lifts that portion of the drapery covering* AGAMEMNON's *face, instantly recognizes it, and then drops the drapery. He recoils down the staircase. Once on the ground, he slowly stands erect and takes a step or two backward. His spear assumes the horizontal position with his arm held back for thrusting. He aims the spear point at* CLYTEMNESTRA's *chest.*

CLYTEMNESTRA *smiles, walks halfway down the staircase, and throws her arms wide open to make his aim easier. Then she continues to descend to the foot of the staircase, the spear point tracking her all the way.*

After a moment, amazed and taken with her courage and power, the SOLDIER

*succumbs. His spear assumes the upright
resting position, and he goes down on one
knee and bows his head before her.*

The other SOLDIERS *do the same.*
CLYTEMNESTRA *is victorious.* AGAMEM-
NON's SOLDIERS *have become* CLYTEMNES-
TRA's. *After a moment, having demon-
strated their allegiance to* CLYTEMNESTRA,
the SOLDIERS *rise and assume strategic stations of defense around the courtyard.
Each soldier holds his spear in one of two
ways: either upright, slightly in front of
him, with elbow flexed, or else in his right
hand, right arm [spear-arm] fully outstretched laterally, away from his body,
the spear's butt against the outside of his
right foot.*

CLYTEMNESTRA *ascends the stairs and
stands at the head of the staircase facing
all triumphantly. The* CHORUS *watches the
entire transaction in disbelief and fear.*)

CLYTEMNESTRA : (*calmly, to the* CHORUS, *as if nothing had intervened*)
1401   You speak to me
as if I were an ordinary woman.
Really, people,
my heart does not flutter
as I talk to you.
You know that.
You can praise or blame me
as you wish;
it is all the same to me.

(*turning and pointing*)
That man is Agamemnon,
my husband.

(*turning to the* CHORUS)
He is dead,
the work of this right hand,
(*holding her right hand up high*)
a master craftsman of Justice.

And that is that.

LEADER: Woman,
            what poisonous plant on earth,
            what potion from the flowing sea
            could you have tasted
            to exhibit such brutality?

CHORUS: The people detest you
            for what you have chopped down
            and thrown away.

            Well,
            now we shall throw you out,

            (*in unison*)
            so hated are you
            by the people.

CLYTEMNESTRA: So!
            It is I
            whom you doom
            and cast from this land,
            hatred heaped upon me,
            curses roaring in my ears!

            But what of the dead man?
            What did you do
            when —
            with no more thought
            than if
            he were about to kill

an animal
from all his pastures
deep in fleece —
he slaughtered
his own child,
of all my children
the one dearest to me,
to charm away
the winds of Thrace?

Were you not bound
to drive him from this land
for the guilt stain on him?

But you did nothing.
Yet,
you hear what I have done,
and suddenly
you are stern judges.

1420   Well, I say to you:
Go on and threaten me.
But remember!
(*pointing to the soldiers*)
Should you acquire the same force,
I am prepared for your rule,
(*sardonically*)
if you can beat me.
Should God grant otherwise,
however,
you shall be taught —
too late, I fear —
good sense.

LEADER: (*defiantly*)
You are cunning beyond measure,
and you are proud,
and murder has made you mad,

that's clear.

CHORUS : (*continuing defiantly*)
        I see the blood
        within your eyes.

        Without honor,
        without friend,
        you shall receive
        stroke for stroke.

CLYTEMNESTRA : (*angrily*)
        Now listen to me!
        (*matter-of-factly*)
        You shall learn the cause
        behind this sacrament:
        I sacrificed this man
        to accomplish Justice
        for my child
        in the names
        of Ruin and Vengeance!

        I do not pace
        the palace floor in fear;
        for Aegisthus —
        stout shield! —
        faithful to me now as before,
        shall keep my fireplace burning!

        (*ascending the staircase, pointing to*
        AGAMEMNON, *scornfully*)
1438   Look at him!
        The lady-killer![40] —
        who satisfied
        all the young virgins
        of Troy!

        (*pointing scornfully to* CASSANDRA)

And her!
Captive of his spear —
and oracle!
Partner in his bed —
and prophet!
Faithful mistress —
and yet,
against her breast
she knew the feel
of a sailor's chest![41]

(*dropping her arm, turning and facing the*
CHORUS)
Their reward is not unworthy.

(*turning to the corpses, pointing to*
AGAMEMNON)
Look at him!

(*pointing to* CASSANDRA)
And her lying next to him —
so skilled in revelation
she even sang her own swan song!

(*pointing to* AGAMEMNON)
Look at him —
the great lover!

(*pointing to* CASSANDRA)
And her — this luxury
that he brought home
for my bed!

LEADER : Oh, for a swift death,
free of the pain and lingering
of the sick,
sleep never ending,
now that our king is gone,

our shield,
kindest of men,
who, for a woman's sake,
suffered so much,
only to be struck down
in the end
by a woman.

CHORUS : O Helen! —
          lovesickness! —
          all the deaths you caused
          single-handedly! —

          oh, so many,
          so very many,
          beneath the walls of Troy.

          (*pointing to the tub*)
          This is your crowning glory!

          And as long as men shall live,
          you will be remembered —
          for who can wash out blood? —
          as a symbol of strife in this home
          and conqueror of its lord
          in days gone by.

CLYTEMNESTRA : (*matter-of-factly*)
1462   How depressing to pray for death!
          How silly to blame Helen
          for slaying single-handedly
          all the Greeks we mourn,
          causing this grief
          beyond all healing!

LEADER : O the Demon
          that crushes this House
          containing descendants of Tantalus![42]

CHORUS: You have given
like-minded women[43]
the daring
that is tearing out
my heart.

Look how hatefully
she hovers
over the corpse,
like a raven,
as she caws
her victory song.

CLYTEMNESTRA : Ah!
Now you've invoked the right spirit —
Demon Vengeance,
who lives in this family
and has gorged himself three times.[44]
From this spirit we inherit
our love of drinking blood.
Before the old wound
has time enough to heal,
it bleeds anew.

1481   PROPHET : Monstrous and heavy is
the Demon that haunts this House!
And you tell a terrible story
of disaster without end.

O God! Almighty Zeus!
Everything from Zeus!
Zeus, who causes everything
and brings about everything.
What can happen without God?
What comes to fulfillment
without Him?

CHORUS: Oh, my king, dearest king,
              how shall I weep for you?
              What do I say from a loving heart?
              You were caught
              in a spider's web,
              and you died a shameful death,
              stabbed with a dagger
              as you lay in your bath,
              by the treacherous hand
              of your queen.

1497   CLYTEMNESTRA : How can you say
              I did this?
              There is no way
              you can say
              this was done
              by Agamemnon's queen.

              (*She pulls out the dagger from* AGAMEM-
              NON's *corpse and holds it up high.*)
              Vengeance did this![45]
              (*looking at the knife*)
              How sharp his sting!
              (*looking at the* CHORUS)
              He has grown old
              remembering Atreus,
              who entertained here
              so gruesomely.
              It was the Demon Vengeance
              who entered me,
              the corpse's queen,
              and sacrificed that man
              for children who were slaughtered!
              (*pantomiming plunging the dagger back
              into the corpse, dropping the dagger into
              the tub, then standing upright, gracefully
              displaying her bloody arms*)

CHORUS: How can we swear
that you are innocent?
How? How?
Still, perhaps you are
that Demon's tool.
From the father,[46]
the monster
found its way to kindred blood,
where it streamed and streamed
until the God of Slaughter found
the right instrument[47]
to win requital
for the children,
covered with gore,
who were eaten.

CHORUS: Oh, my king, dearest king,
how shall I weep for you?
What do I say from a loving heart?
You were caught
in a spider's web,
and you died a shameful death,
stabbed with a dagger
as you lay in your bath,
by the treacherous hand
of your queen.

1521   CLYTEMNESTRA : There was nothing shameful
in his death.
As for treachery,
did he not bring death
into our house?

I dealt
with him
as he dealt
with the child of our love,
Iphigenia,

who weeps tears endlessly.

And he had better watch his words
in the underworld.
With the knife he slew.
With the knife he was slain.

CHORUS: I am helpless and bereft.

I am overwhelmed.

What should I do
when, on all sides,
the House is caving in?

I fear the beating,
bloody rain —
drizzle turns to hurricane! —
breaking down
the House.

So! Fate,
in the name of Justice,
continues to grind her axe
for still more crimes of horror.

1540   LEADER: Dear land, sweet earth,
could you not have buried me
before I saw this man lie dead
within a silver tub?

(SOLDIERS *carry* CASSANDRA *'s corpse behind the scenes. They then lift* AGAMEM-
NON*'s corpse from the tub and carry it
down the staircase and downstage.*[48]
*They lay the corpse neatly supine, hands
at the sides, and reverently cover it with a
drapery, face exposed.*

The palace doors close.
The tub is removed from behind the
scenes.
The LEADER *continues:*)

Who will bury him?
Who will mourn?

(*turning to* CLYTEMNESTRA)
Will you dare,
you who killed your lord?
Will you dare make lamentation?
Will you render sacrament
defiled by loathsome crimes?
Will you deliver the eulogy
with the tears
of a true heart's grief
over this great man's grave?

CLYTEMNESTRA :   (*angrily, still at the head of the*
           staircase)
           How dare you say such things!
           By us he fell,
           by us he died,
           and we shall bury him!
           But there will be no tears.

           Only his child,
           Iphigenia,
           will run to greet her father —
           as a daughter should —
           on the banks
           of the swift river of sorrow,
           and throw her arms around him
           and kiss him.

PROPHET :   (*moving slowly downstage to the corpse,*
           then speaking)

1560
Victor today —
vanquished tomorrow.
The killer is killed.
Anger for anger.

Justice is impossible
to attain!

And yet,
this truth stands eternal
at the throne of God:
"Whoever does evil must pay."
That is the law.

Then who can ever break a curse?
Humanity is destined for destruction.

CLYTEMNESTRA :   (*nodding in agreement, to the*
PROPHET)
For once you've predicted the future![49]

(*descending the staircase and walking up
to the corpse*)
As for me, I call a truce
with the Demon in this House.
I am willing to forget —
hard though it is —
everything he's done,
if only —
from now on —
he goes far away
and bleeds to death
other palaces
in other lands.

I shall be content
keeping but few of my treasures,
if only I can keep my household clean

of the madness
of murder for murder.

(AEGISTHUS *enters from the audience.   On
discovering the corpse,   he slowly walks
around it,   this way and that,   staring intently at it.   At last believing his eyes,   he
smiles triumphantly.*

He takes CLYTEMNESTRA *'s bloody
hands in his own and kisses them.   He tenderly rubs her hands against his neck and
cheeks,   leaving bloodstains there.   They
smile warmly at each other.   He kisses her
passionately on the lips.   Then he bounds
to the head of the staircase.*)

AEGISTHUS :   (*turning, joyously*)
1577   What a glorious day,
            O day of retribution!

            It warms my heart
            to see this man before me here
            caught in a net
            woven by the Furies,
            paying in full
            for his father's crime!
            At last I can say
            the gods in heaven
            look down and avenge
            the sufferings of men on earth!

            (*beginning to descend the staircase*)
            Atreus,
            this man's (*pointing to* AGAMEMNON)
            father, king of this land,
            banished his brother,
            Thyestes,
            my father,

from his home
and from his nation,
when Thyestes challenged
Atreus' right as king.

Time passed.
My father returned,
begging forgiveness.
And, indeed,
he was well received.

Atreus,
this man's (*pointing to* AGAMEMNON)
godless father,
playing the good host,
prepared a feast of celebration.

It was a festive day
full of good cheer.
But the carved slices of meat
my father was served
were the flesh of his own children!
Atreus had cut off the fingers and toes
and covered them with larger slices
with no distinguishing features.

This roast he served my father! —
who, giving no thought
to the nature
of the dinner set before him,
ate that gruesome food,
whose curse is working still
before your very eyes!

On realizing
the horrible thing he'd done,
Thyestes vomited the meal
with a cry,

and overturning
the banquet table
to symbolize his curse,
1600   he invoked
this unbearable doom:
"Thus may the House of Atreus
come crashing down in ruin."

(*walking to the corpse*)
That is why you see
this dead man here.

I, along with Justice,
planned this murder —
I, the youngest child
of my poor father,
with him driven into exile,
a helpless babe in arms.
But when I grew up,
Justice
brought me home again.

Even in exile
I followed this man's every move.
I used to dream
every possible scheme
to catch him.

(*turning the corpse over on its belly,
covering it with the drapery,
then straddling it*)
And now that he's caught
in this trap of Justice,
even death for me
would be delicious.
(*running to the head of the staircase,
turning, smiling triumphantly*)

LEADER: Aegisthus!
Such boasting at this time
is vile!
The king is dead —
murdered! —
and your sole role —
you admit it
of your own free will! —
was to *plan* his pitiful end.
I tell you,
there shall be no escape —
first cursing by the people,
then stoning to death!

(*With this threat, the* SOLDIER *nearest the*
LEADER *points his spear at the* LEADER.)

AEGISTHUS: (*with bravado from the head of the*
staircase, to the LEADER)
Look who's talking!
You who shout orders
from the lowest deck
while the captain stands on the bridge!

(*slowly descending*)
1619   You are old, people.
Well, you shall see
how hard it is
at your age
to learn good behavior.

(*The* SOLDIER *with spear leveled at the*
LEADER *moves closer to him, until his*
spear almost touches him. AEGISTHUS *de-*
scends to the foot of the staircase.)
Chains and hunger pains
are wise and excellent teachers.
They can teach good manners

even to the old.

If you still don't understand me,
pay attention!
(*walking up to and pointing to the spears
and touching the tip of the one aimed at
the* LEADER)
Do you see these?
My advice to you is this:
try not to hit these spears.
They hurt!

LEADER: Like a woman,
You waited out the war.
And you shamed the bed
and you planned the death
of our commander in chief.

AEGISTHUS: Keep talking
and you shall be screaming!
Yours is no song of Orpheus,
whose rapturous voice
drew other creatures after him.
Quite the contrary,
your yelping will drag you down,
and force will tame you.

(*All* SOLDIERS *point their spears at members of the* CHORUS.)

LEADER: How can you be king of Argos? —
you who planned the murder
but did not dare to do it —
to kill the king yourself?

AEGISTHUS: Yes, snaring him
was for the queen.
He never trusted me.

He hated me.

But now,
with his gold,
(*strolling amongst the* CHORUS *members fa-
miliarly and placing his hand in cama-
raderie on the shoulders of a few of them*)
I shall begin
to make friends.

Any man with a mind of his own
shall feel the heavy yoke
on his neck.
It means nothing to me.
He shall be no favored colt
prancing about so free.

And hunger —
along with his friend,
the frightening dark —
shall see to it he is trained.

1643   LEADER: Why, you coward,
                could you not
                have slain the man yourself?
                Why did it have to be his wife,
                curse of our country
                and curse of our gods?

                Oh, that Orestes lives!
                Will Fate grown gracious
                bring him home
                to execute these killers?

        AEGISTHUS: You shall learn then,
                since you are so stubborn!
                All right! Men!
                Here's work to be done!

(*All* SOLDIERS *aim their spears at the*
LEADER*'s chest while the other members of*
the CHORUS *withdraw in fear to the periph-*
ery of the courtyard.)

LEADER: (*drawing his sword*)
We all have swords!

AEGISTHUS: (*drawing his sword*)
I, too, have a sword.
And I am not afraid to die.

LEADER: (*cutting the air with his sword, moving*
toward AEGISTHUS)
Death you say,
and death it shall be!
That fatal word we understand.

(*One* SOLDIER *seizes the* LEADER *from be-*
hind and pulls him backward to the
ground while another SOLDIER *disarms*
him.
    AEGISTHUS, *with* CLYTEMNESTRA *right*
behind him, rushes toward the LEADER,
kneels on one knee, and pulls his sword-
arm back. AEGISTHUS *is about to plunge*
his sword when CLYTEMNESTRA *kneels and*
blocks his arm.)

CLYTEMNESTRA: (*to* AEGISTHUS)
No, my dearest!
No more evil today!
Our harvest is ample.
Our suffering is abundant.
I cannot bear more blood.

(CLYTEMNESTRA *and* AEGISTHUS *stand.*

AEGISTHUS *sheathes his sword.*

The insurrection over, the SOLDIERS *disperse and again assume stations of defense throughout the courtyard.*

The LEADER *stands and brushes himself off. The* SOLDIER *with the* LEADER*'s sword looks at* CLYTEMNESTRA*, who nods, whereupon he returns the sword to him. The* LEADER *sheathes his sword. Then the* SOLDIER *reassumes his station.*

The LEADER *rejoins the* CHORUS*, which has been watching the proceedings in fear.*

CLYTEMNESTRA *walks to the foot of the staircase, then suddenly turns to face the* CHORUS *and the audience.*)

(with uncharacteristic warmth)
My dear old friends,
go home.
Accept your fate.
Do not ask for trouble.

What we did
we had to do.

Let us hope
this is the end
of our suffering.
Then, crushed as we are
by the brutal heel of Fate,
we can still accept it.

Try to understand,
even though
I am only a woman.

AEGISTHUS : *(childishly)*

1662
> But what about these fools —
> their leering gibes,
> and the way they've heckled me,
> tempting Fate?
> They discredit
> everything I say
> and mock me
> and my fitness to be king.

LEADER: (*defiantly*)
> It was never our way
> to lick a coward's feet.

AEGISTHUS: (*to the* LEADER, *shaking his fist*)
> Wait! I'll get you yet!

CHORUS: (*defiantly*)
> Unless God's guiding hand
> brings Orestes home again!

AEGISTHUS: (*with bravado*)
> Exiles thrive on hope.
> I know.
> Once I was one.

CHORUS: Keep on!

> Grow fat!

> Soil justice while you can!

AEGISTHUS: Rest assured —
> you shall pay the price
> for this stupidity!

LEADER: Crow and strut, brave cock,
> as long as you're near your hen!

CLYTEMNESTRA : (*to* AEGISTHUS, *angrily*)
>   Stop it, I say!
>   Asses bray,
>   and *you* listen?

> (AEGISTHUS, *wounded by her words, turns to face her. She takes his hands in hers and smiles. Then she speaks calmly and comfortingly.*)

>   But you are lord and master here!
>   (AEGISTHUS *smiles.*)

1673

>   (*reassuringly and confidently*)
>   Come!
>   Together
>   we shall put our house in order.

> (CLYTEMNESTRA *turns with* AEGISTHUS *to face the palace. She links her right arm in his left. Then, slowly and majestically, they ascend the staircase.*
>   *The palace doors open.*
>   CLYTEMNESTRA *and* AEGISTHUS *enter.*
>   *The palace doors slowly close.*
>   *The* CHORUS *looks on in despair.*
>   *Darkness descends.*)

THE END

EPILOGUE

NARRATOR: Agamemnon's unbridled ambition, greed, and thirst for glory end in his own death, and tyranny continues to rule his nation.

In the next play of the trilogy, the blood-for-blood chain of personal vengeance continues. Clytemnestra and Aegisthus fall to the vengeful blade of Clytemnestra's son, Orestes. But who will bring vengeance upon Orestes?

In the final play, Athena, the Goddess of Wisdom, brings an end to personal vengeance. She establishes a civilized way of attaining justice by means of the court of law, which is impartial and brings finality and closure. Orestes is exonerated, and the curse on the House of Atreus is broken.

Incidentally, whatever happened to Helen, the cause of the Trojan War? She and her husband Menelaus found their way back to Greece, where they lived happily ever after.

MAP OF AGAMEMNON'S WORLD

THRACE

Troy (Ilium)

Simois River

Scamander River

▲ Mt. Ida

Lemnos
(Rock of Hermes)

Sea

This map is diagrammatic and not to scale.   The
distance from Troy to Mt. Athos is about 100 miles.
Several locations are unknown (indicated by question
marks) and have been reconstructed from the Greek
text. The Cocytus River and the Acheron River are
not on the map because they are in the underworld.
The dotted lines connect the series of eight
beacons from Troy to Argos (see pp. 58-63).

THREE GENERATIONS OF MAJOR CHARACTERS

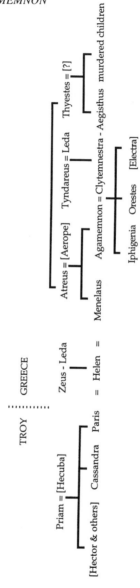

= marriage
- liaison without marriage
[ ] not mentioned in *AGAMEMNON*

The same Leda is the mother of both Helen and Clytemnestra.

PRONUNCIATION GUIDE
For American English

a	as in *apple*
ack	as in *back*
air	as in *hair*
al	as in *pal*
an	as in *fan*
ank	as in *bank*
ar	as in *car*
ass	as in *pass*
aw	as in *awful*
ay	as in *day*
ch	as in *chin*
e	as in *bed*
ee	as in *bee*
er	as in *runner*
ess	as in *less*
eye	as in *eye*
g	as in *gun*
i	as in *pit*
iss	as in *kiss*
j	as in *jam*
o	as in *hot*
oh	as in *toe*
oo	as in *zoo*
or	as in *for*
oy	as in *boy*
s, ss	as in *sit* (not as in *rays*)
th	as in *think* (not as in *that*)
u, uh	as in *sun*
uss	as in *fuss*
y (vowel) as in *try*	
y (initial consonant) as in *yellow*	
z	as in *zoo*

(Accent the syllable in CAPITALS.)

Acheron	A kuh ron
Aegean	ee JEE un
Aegisthus	ee JISS thuss
Aegyplanctus	EE jee PLANK tuss
Aeschylus	ESS kuh luss (EESS kuh luss, *British*)
Agamemnon	AG uh MEM non
Arachneos	uh rack NEE oss
Argos	AR goss
Artemis	AR tuh miss
Asopos	uh SO poss
Athos	A thoss
Atreus	AY tree uss
Aulis	AW liss
Calchas	KAL kuss
Cassandra	kuh SAN druh (*not* kuh SAHN druh)
Chalcis	KAL siss
Cithaeron	SITH ee ron

Clytemnestra	KLY tem NESS truh
Cocytus	koh SY tuss (*not* koh SEE tuss)
Cronus	KROH nuss
Delphi	DELL fy (*not* DELL fee)
Euripus	yuh RIP uss
Gorgopis	gor GOP iss
Helen	HELL un
Hermes	HER meez
Ida	EYE duh
Ilium	ILL ee um
Iphigenia	IF uh juh NY uh
Itys	EE tiss
Leda	LEE duh
Lemnos	LEM noss
Macistos	MA siss toss
Menelaus	MEN uh LAY uss
Messapion	muh SAP ee on
Orestea/Oresteia	oh REST ee uh
Orestes	oh REST eez

Orpheus	OR fee uss
Paris	PAIR iss
Phocis	FOH siss
Pleiades	PLEE uh deez
Priam	PRY um (*not* PREE um)
Saronic	suh RON ik
Scamander	skuh MAN der
Scylla	SILL uh
Simois	SIM oh iss (*not* SIM WAH)
Strophius	STROH fee uss
Strymon	STRY mun
Tantalus	TAN tuh luss
Thrace	THRAYSS
Thyestes	thy ESS teez
Trojan	TROH juhn
Troy	TROY
Tyndareus	tin DAIR ee uss
Uranus	yuh RAY nuss
Zeus	ZOOSS

NOTES

[1] line numbering (p. 37).

The line numbers appearing in the left margins of this translation run from 1 through 1673. They refer to the line numbers of the Greek text of *AGAMEMNON* contained in the Loeb Classical Library edition (Smyth, *Aeschylus II*) and are provided only to help those who wish to compare the translation with the Greek. They do not correspond to the line numbers of this translation, which are not given, because the Greek and English lines are not of equivalent length or number.

[2] "shelter" (p. 37).

Aeschylus uses a Greek word whose generic meaning is *shelter, a covering from the rain,* or *the roof over one's head.* In a specific sense it may mean any sheltered or covered structure including a tent, house, palace, or roof-covered terrace.

In addition to the word's literal meaning, the context tells us that the word is referring to a sheltered part of the palace compound. For example, the sentry complains of things that make his work drudgery, but significantly he does not complain of exposure to sun or rain. However, he does complain of his "dew-drenched bed," which suggests that his shelter, although covered above, is open at the sides. A roof-covered terrace would provide shelter from sun and rain but not from dew. Therefore, I have translated the word with its generic meaning *shelter*, and I have identified that shelter in the set as a roof-covered terrace.

Curiously, in other translations of *AGAMEMNON*, the word is mistranslated as *roof* (or *roofs*), in the sense of a rooftop on which to stand — an observation deck. Perhaps these translators abandoned the word's literal meaning because they assumed that a rooftop was a better place than the ground for the sentry to observe the distant mountaintop, which was his task. Although a rooftop is a better position from which to observe things approaching from the ground — because height extends the horizon — a rooftop would offer no significant advantage over the ground for the purpose of sighting a nearby mountaintop, elevated well above the horizon. (Readers who find this counterintuitive might wish to test it in a site where the topography is comparable.)

3 "Apollo, Pan, or Zeus" (p. 43).

This is the first mention of any of the gods by name, and what a curious collection of gods it is! Apollo and Zeus are not surprising, because they are major deities who are invoked repeatedly throughout the play — but why Pan? Why does the chorus mention this minor woodland deity and ignore the goddess Artemis, the major woodland deity, who in just a short time will figure so prominently in the play?

I suggest that Aeschylus deliberately mentions Pan because he is showing us at the onset that the gods one invokes, at least where wild animals are concerned, are arbitrary, an entirely personal matter, and that a great evil is about to take place in the name of Artemis.

4 "Neither sacrifices . . . nor libations . . . can soften the inexorable anger of God" (p. 44).

Aeschylus is telling us that sacrifice — any sacrifice, not only human — is ineffective to appease angry gods. Later the chorus tells us that the sacrifice of Iphigenia was wanton murder. As the play progresses, Aeschylus tells us that sacrifice is not only ineffective, it is evil.

Among the ancient Greeks, Aeschylus was a religious radical on the subject of sacrifice — not only human sacrifice, which had been abandoned in Athens by the time Aeschylus lived there in the fifth century B.C., but also animal sacrifice, which was still actively practiced. Aeschylus was against sacrifice in any form.

Scholars have noted similarities between Aeschylus' conception of Zeus and the conception of God by some of the Hebrew prophets, citing biblical passages such as "God does not desire sacrifice" (Psalm 40:6) and "I desire mercy and not sacrifice" (Hosea 6:6).

5a–e "I am a master at chanting prophecies. . . . That same power let me interpret the omen of the birds and send the brother-kings . . . on to the land of Troy. . . . Two eagles . . . omen for kings of ships . . . caught a hare. . . . Pregnant . . . she was ripped wide open!" (p. 47).

By speaking these words, the prophet of the chorus identifies himself as Calchas, because it was Calchas, the prophet of the Greek army, who interpreted the "omen of the birds," which led to the sacrifice of Iphigenia.

6a–e "Here is my interpretation: "Not two birds, but the two warrior sons of Atreus . . . were feeding on that hare! . . . [T]his carnage shall take place in Troy. . . . The virgin Artemis is angry. . . . She hates the eagles' feast" (p. 48).

In this speech Calchas, the prophet, repeats and expands upon his interpretation of the omen of the birds: The two eagles symbolize the brother-kings Agamemnon and Menelaus, while the pregnant hare, ripped open and fed upon by the eagles, symbolizes Troy, destroyed by the two kings. The goddess Artemis, protector of wild animals, is angry at the eagles for their feast — and presumably at Agamemnon and Menelaus for their plans to destroy Troy.

7a–b "O Apollo . . . Do not let Artemis punish the Greeks with endless foul winds, making sailing impossible" (p. 49).

In this speech Calchas, the prophet, associates the eagles' feast with the "foul wind" that prevented the Greek army from sailing to

Troy. He explains that Artemis, in her anger at Agamemnon and Menelaus, has punished the Greeks by creating an unfavorable wind so they cannot sail to Troy.

As prophet of the Greek army, Calchas calls upon Apollo to stop Artemis' efforts. In the polytheistic religion of the Greeks, the gods did not act in a concerted way but were often at odds. Therefore, a person could invoke one god in the hopes of neutralizing the actions of another.

8a–c "O Zeus! . . . the Victory of Zeus! . . . And from our pain . . . comes a divine gift — Wisdom" (pp. 50–51).

The leader of the chorus delivers this speech, sometimes called the Victory of Zeus hymn, which celebrates the triumph of Zeus over his father, Cronus. According to Aeschylus in *AGAMEM-NON*, Zeus was a god who cared about human beings, whereas Cronus was not. In his caring, Zeus gave people the great gift of understanding that wisdom comes through suffering.

Aeschylus has placed the Victory hymn just before his description of the sacrifice of Iphigenia. That sacrifice — like all human sacrifice — brought suffering to the Greeks. However, because wisdom comes from suffering, Aeschylus gives meaning to Iphigenia's sacrificial death and provides a theological balm to his audience for their own past, present, or future suffering. This is an example of Aeschylus' religious philosophy, original with him.

9 "The foul wind was caused by Bad Luck" (p. 52).

The narrator reports that when the storm first came up, no one — including Agamemnon — attached any significance to it other than bad luck. Compare with note 11.

10 "[T]he Greek army hungered at Aulis, across the straits from the shores at Chalcis" (p. 52).

The straits mentioned here are the straits of Euripus, which have the same name today. Agamemnon and the Greek army sailed through these straits into the Aegean Sea en route to Troy.

Aulis is a town located on the southwestern shore of the straits of Euripus. Aulis was the gathering place of the Greek soldiers and also the place where Iphigenia was sacrificed. Chalcis is a town on the northeastern shore of the straits, opposite Aulis. (See "Map of Agamemnon's World," pp. 172–73).

[11] "Then, to calm the wind, the prophet, blaming Artemis, proposed another means, worse than the bitter storm" (p. 52).

Here the narrator describes how Calchas endowed the storm with religious significance, thereby changing a commonplace natural event into divine punishment for the Greeks, sent by the angry Artemis. Compare with note 9 above.

Even if one were to endow the foul wind with religious significance, the reasonable religious interpretation would be that Artemis did not want the Greeks to sail to Troy and destroy it, so she sent the foul wind to prevent their sailing. However, Calchas ignored this reasonable interpretation and replaced it with a distorted one. He told Agamemnon that Artemis would be appeased and would calm the foul wind so that the Greeks could sail to Troy and destroy it if only Agamemnon would sacrifice his daughter Iphigenia.

Could anyone believe that Artemis, so horrified by the death of a hare, would not be equally — or more — horrified by the death of a beautiful young girl? Calchas' twisted interpretation of the omen illustrates Aeschylus' scorn for the religious establishment of his time, which endowed commonplace natural events with unreasonable religious significance that had deadly consequences for the innocent.

Aeschylus clearly does not have a high opinion of Calchas. Unlike Homer, he does not have Calchas sail to Troy with the Greek army. Instead, the prophet has remained at home in Argos with the rest of the old folks. Aeschylus does not even make Calchas a separate character in the play. Minimizing Calchas' importance by making him a member of the chorus allowed Aeschylus to attack him obliquely and anonymously, which was much safer than direct criticism in a religious culture that held prophets, especially Calchas, in high esteem. Aeschylus' life had already been threatened for revealing some of the secrets of the mystery religion (see "Religious Philosophy," pp. 7–8). He could hardly risk getting into trouble again by directly attacking Calchas.

12a–b "Agamemnon spoke these words: 'Fate will be angry if I do not obey [Calchas], and angry if I sacrifice this child. . . . Whatever I do is wrong! Yet, how can I fail fleet and friends? They urge sacrifice of innocent blood, and that is just" (p. 53).

I have translated the Greek word *ananke* (necessity) as "Fate."

The narrator describes Agamemnon as saying that Fate has given him an impossible choice — to sacrifice his child and sail to Troy, or not to sacrifice his child and not sail to Troy. Agamemnon's friends, the host of soldiers, are impatient and restless. They urge human sacrifice. That is "just," Agamemnon says. He will do what his friends — and Fate — want. Thus, Agamemnon rationalizes the sacrifice of his daughter. Aeschylus thereby shows that politically ambitious people may use religious interpretation and their own rationalizations to further their own self-serving goals.

13a–b "He blamed it all on Fate! Look how unbridled ambition twisted his mind! . . . Now his will would stop at nothing. . . . Agamemnon took it upon himself to make his daughter the first sacrifice for the sake of ships!" (pp. 53–54).

Agamemnon blamed Fate for his decision to sacrifice Iphigenia, but the narrator reminds us that Agamemnon "took it upon himself" to kill his child. Agamemnon was led by his "unbridled ambition" and was solely responsible for his murderous decision.

Agamemnon probably was not the first father to sacrifice his child in order to satisfy personal ambition, and he certainly was not the last. Fathers who behave in this manner possess what I call an "Agamemnon complex." Tussman has written, "Who does not know an ambitious or dedicated man — or woman — who has sacrificed a child on the altar of a career? Our world teems with Agamemnons" (*The Burden of Office*, p. 14).

[14] "the third cup of wine" (p. 55).

At a Greek banquet or religious festival, the first cup of wine was dedicated to all the Olympian gods, the second cup to the dead heroes in the underworld, and the third cup to Zeus the Savior. Zeus is not mentioned in the Greek text — probably because the ancient Athenian audience would have understood the reference.

[15] "I could not watch what happened next, and I cannot bear to talk about it" (p. 55).

The narrator says that he watched all the proceedings leading up to the sacrifice of Iphigenia, but he could not bring himself to witness the execution itself. Furthermore, he cannot bear to talk about it even now, ten years after the event. Why couldn't he watch it then, and why can't he speak of it now? Because the throat-slitting of an innocent and beautiful young girl is too horrible to watch or recount.

The narrator concludes with a snide remark about Calchas and his art: "But the art of Calchas never fails" (p. 55). The art of Calchas *never fails* because the victim always dies. Moreover, the storm died with Iphigenia, did it not?

Pindar, Aeschylus' contemporary, was the first to write of the sacrifice of Iphigenia. Aeschylus tells the story as Pindar did.

A new playwright, Euripides, appeared in the generation after Aeschylus. Euripides went even further than Aeschylus in revealing abhorrence of the sacrifice of Iphigenia. Aeschylus only intimates that Artemis does not approve of Calchas' call for the death of Iphigenia, but Euripides demonstrates the goddess's disapproval in his two plays *Iphigenia in Aulis* and *Iphigenia among the Taurians*.

In Euripides' plays, at the instant of Iphigenia's sacrifice, the Greek soldiers hear the sound of the slitting of a throat. But when they look upon the slain victim, they see that a miracle has occurred. Instead of Iphigenia, a deer with a slit throat lies there! The gods, including Artemis, have swooped down at the last instant, rescued Iphigenia from the altar, and substituted the deer in her place.

Subsequent writers followed either the version of Pindar and Aeschylus or the version of Euripides. Vergil, the greatest of the Latin poets, writing in the first century B.C., four centuries after Aeschylus, followed the Pindar-Aeschylus version. Alluding to the sacrifice of Iphigenia in the second book of the *Aeneid*, Vergil writes: "O Greeks, you appeased the winds by the blood of a murdered virgin before you came to the shores of Troy."

Bulfinch's *Mythology* (New York: Thomas Y. Crowell Company, 1970), the standard American reference for over a century, does not tell the Pindar-Aeschylus version; Bulfinch speaks only of Euripides' version — Iphigenia's rescue by the intervention of the gods. The reader who prepares to read or see *AGAMEMNON* by reading Bulfinch will, therefore, be thoroughly confused. Hamilton's *Mythology* (see Selected Sources) tells both the Pindar-Aeschylus and the Euripides versions.

The purpose of this note is twofold: to show the variation between the ancient writers in telling the mythological stories, and also to make sure the reader is not confused about which version is related in *AGAMEMNON*. In Aeschylus' *AGAMEMNON*, Iphigenia is sacrificed.

[16] "To the first runner and to the last goes the victory!" (p. 62).

In this breathtaking metaphor in Clytemnestra's Beacon speech (pp. 58–63), Aeschylus transforms eight successive stationary bonfires on mountaintops between Troy and Greece (see "Map of Agamemnon's World," pp. 172–73) into a thrilling relay race in which runners carry torches and pass them on as they do at the opening of the modern Olympic Games. The eight mountains are Ida, rock of Hermes, Athos, Macistos, Messapion, Cithaeron, Aegyplanctus, and Arachneos.

In this metaphor, however, there is only one relay team, so, strictly speaking, there can be no winner. However, because this team brings such extraordinary news — that the Greeks have won the Trojan War — Clytemnestra says there is not only one winner but two! "To the first runner and to the last goes the victory!" (p. 62). Who are these two victorious runners?

The first runner — i.e., bonfire or beacon — is easy to identify: the God of Fire or those Greeks in Troy who kindled the first fire.

But who is the last runner? Is it the eighth beacon, on top of Mt. Arachneos, so visible to the palace of Agamemnon? Or is there a ninth runner?

When Clytemnestra receives news of the beacon burning on Mt. Arachneos, she immediately commands that torches be lighted everywhere in Argos. These torches are Clytemnestra's. She is the last runner.

[17] "Ilium" (p. 70).

"Ilium" is a synonym for Troy. Homer's *Iliad* concerns the War at Ilium or the War at Troy, more commonly known as the Trojan War.

[18] "free . . . from knowledge of coloring bronze" (p. 83).

Clytemnestra is being cryptically ironic. Bronze is a metal and resists dyeing. On the other hand, a bronze blade will easily turn red when it is used to stab someone. Clytemnestra may be "free . . . from knowledge of coloring bronze" while she delivers this line, but she expects to have full knowledge of it very shortly.

[19] "Helen. Hell! Hell on ships and hell on men and hell on cities" (p. 89).

The *Helen/Hell on* pun exists in the Greek as well as in the English. In Greek, the prefix *hel-* means *destruction*, and Aeschylus lists the things Helen has destroyed: ships, men, and cities.

Hell, serendipitously, exists in the English language and enables the pun to be translated almost literally.

[20] "those who beached their boat in the leafy shade of the banks of the river Simois" (p. 89).

"Those" refers to Paris, Helen, and their retinue.

The river Simois was the second major river of Troy. The first was the Scamander.

Aeschylus conjures up a lovely place in Troy where Paris and Helen disembark: a peaceful place, quiet and secluded, the kind of place where lovers like to meet, but a place, we realize, whose loveliness will soon be annihilated by war. This is an example of Aeschylus' startling — chilling, in this case — contrasts.

[21] "the ballot box of blood" (p. 96).

Agamemnon's metaphor is of the gods voting in the style of Athenians. In Greek democracy, Greeks voted, but not by secret ballot. There was a separate ballot box for each candidate or point of view. Greek jurors also voted in this way. In a murder trial, after the twelve jurors made up their minds regarding condemnation or acquittal, they dropped their ballots (pebbles or other tokens) into separate boxes (urns) labeled with the choices — not into a single box receiving different choices. Of course, everyone could see how everyone else voted.

In this metaphor, the Olympian gods (also twelve) were passing judgment on the fate of Troy. Agamemnon states that all the gods dropped their ballots in "the ballot box of blood" (p. 96) as opposed to the ballot box of survival, by which he means that Troy was unanimously condemned to annihilation by the gods. However, mythology teaches that the gods did not unanimously condemn Troy. Several of the gods — most notably Apollo and Aphrodite — loved Troy and tried to protect it. Agamemnon is exaggerating greatly to justify his annihilation of Troy.

22a–b "Regarding other matters — our nation, and whether we are all worshiping the gods the same way — we shall . . . find out what is healthy. . . .   As for that which needs a cure, we shall . . . remove the corruption" (p. 99).

Agamemnon says he intends to examine the current state of the nation and also its religion. His concern about the government is understandable— he is, after all, the ruler who has been absent for ten years. However, his concern about monolithic polytheism may be surprising to many today who have assumed that monolithic religion is the exclusive province of the monotheistic religions. Intolerance of variations in religious thought is very ancient, indeed.

23 "A father's only son!" (p. 104).

Clytemnestra is speaking figuratively. Literally, Agamemnon's father had two sons, Agamemnon and Menelaus. Clytemnestra does not have this literal meaning in mind but rather the figurative one: When a father has only one son, that son is particularly precious.

24 "draperies" (p. 105).

Aeschylus uses several Greek words that describe three categories of fabrics: *spreads* such as bedspreads; *covers* such as table-cloths, cloaks, robes, or carpets; and *hangings* such as embroideries, tapestries, curtains, or draperies. Such variety of description may have pleased Athenian audiences, but it confuses English-speaking ones and makes translation difficult. I have chosen the word *draperies* to represent all three categories. My choice is based on the following:

The context provides clues that allow us to narrow the possibilities: Agamemnon is about to express reluctance to trample upon these fabrics because they are objects of great value and beauty and they are not meant to be walked upon (pp. 106–8). Later we shall learn from Clytemnestra (pp. 145–46) that the fabric is supple, can be cast like a fishing net, is light enough for one woman to cast, is strong enough to entrap a strong man, and is easily penetrated by a knife.

The fabrics in the play cannot be carpets because carpets are heavy and are not easily penetrated by a knife. Most importantly, carpets are meant to be trampled upon, and the fabrics depicted are not.

They cannot be embroideries or tapestries because those are densely woven and stiff, not supple. Moreover, they would be too unwieldy for a single person to cast like a fishing net. Furthermore, they would not easily admit a thrusted knife, but on the contrary would shield against it. Most importantly, they would not ensnare a victim as would a fishing net, to use Clytemnestra's image (pp. 145–46), or "a spider's web," to use the chorus's phrase (p. 155).

The fabrics cannot be cloaks or robes because they would not make a smooth path between the chariot and the palace. On the contrary, they would present a messy appearance and create stumbling blocks to anyone who walked upon them. Moreover, there is something almost comical about clothing lying on the ground because it reminds us of an adolescent's bedroom. Messiness and clumsiness, and the comedy they create, are the very opposite of the scene that Aeschylus is conveying here.

Bedspreads, tablecloths, curtains, or lightweight draperies would serve the requirements of the play. But of these choices, only draperies both look majestic and have a majestic-sounding name. Only the statement "Lay the draperies upon the ground" inspires awe. Furthermore, only draperies could actually serve a useful function throughout the play. Curiously, the word *draperies* is one of the words missing from Liddell and Scott's *Greek-English Lexicon*. Incidentally, R. P. Winnington-Ingram, an Aeschylus scholar, also likes the word *draperies* in this context (Easterling and Knox, *The Cambridge History of Classical Literature*, p. 34).

Finally, a practical suggestion: At least one of the draperies must be small enough to be managed by one person yet large enough to ensnare Agamemnon by completely covering his bath-tub. The ideal size is about two yards wide by three yards long.

25a–c "crimson . . . many-colored . . . purple" (pp. 105–8).

The Greek text varies in describing the color of the draperies. Aeschylus sometimes uses the adjective *crimson*, at other times *purple*, and still other times *many-colored*. I have kept the varying adjectives because varying colors are realistic and do not create confusion for the reader, unlike the varying nouns described in note 24.

26 "that man who really could raise the dead!" (p. 117).

This is probably an allusion to Aesculapius, a mortal son of the god Apollo. Aesculapius, like his father, was an excellent physician. Impressed by his own healing skills, Aesculapius tried to bring Hippolytus, a young man who had died, back to life. He succeeded. For a mortal to bring another mortal back to life was sacrilegious because it went beyond the limits of mortal medicine. Only the gods were entitled to immortality. Zeus, enraged, hurled a thunderbolt at Aesculapius and killed him.

27 "Fate may clash with Fate" (p. 117).

Although a god opposing a god was commonplace in the ancient Greek religion (see note 7a–b), the ancient Greeks believed that Destiny had an inexorable course because the three Fates, having the same point of view, acted in unison. Here Aeschylus is presenting another radical idea: even Destiny is not inexorable because the three Fates don't always have the same point of view and therefore don't always act in unison. Aeschylus thus wipes out the philosophy of absolute determinism, although his is not an explanation for free will. He only implies that determinism can take more than one path.

28 "If you do not understand . . . make a gesture" (p. 120).

Some scholars have ridiculed this command and this speech of Clytemnestra's. They reason as follows: if, as Clytemnestra suggests, Cassandra is deaf and dumb or knows no Greek, how could Cassandra understand Clytemnestra's command to make a gesture? Therefore, isn't Clytemnestra ridiculous to say these words, and wasn't Aeschylus ridiculous to have crafted them?

Not at all.   Clytemnestra is angry that Cassandra, her new slave, is ignoring her.   This command gives Cassandra one last chance to respond and appease Clytemnestra's anger.   But Cassandra remains silent.   She does nothing, thereby showing Clytemnestra that Cassandra, her slave, is in control of the moment. This, of course, enrages Clytemnestra even more.

The deaf and dumb perceive attempts at communication with them and do in fact gesticulate to indicate their disability. Similarly, a foreigner who does not speak a new country's language also gesticulates to indicate an inability to speak the language.   We shall soon learn that Cassandra is not deaf and dumb and that she knows Greek — "too good, I think" (p. 134).

Clytemnestra correctly concludes that Cassandra, by ignoring her, is either emotionally disturbed ("She is mad," p. 120) or is deliberately provoking her ("I have no more time for her contempt," p. 121).   Clytemnestra's command and speech are therefore highly dramatic and effective — illustrative, too, of Aeschylus' profound understanding of human psychology.

[29] "She, once partner in his bed, now partner in his murder" (p. 124).

Clytemnestra has changed not only partners, but partnership roles.   Once she was Agamemnon's partner in bed, but no longer. Now she is Aegisthus' partner, both in bed and in planning Agamemnon's murder.

[30] "What good is prophecy? Such skill in words is evil, terrifying those who learn the future" (p. 126).

This disdain of prophecy is another of Aeschylus' radical ideas.

[31] "Oh, for the nightingale's song and a fate like hers!" (p. 126).

In mythology, the nightingale once was a woman who suffered terrible personal losses. When she was about to be murdered, the gods, out of pity, transformed her into a nightingale.

The chorus finds Cassandra's fate similar, but Cassandra disagrees. She finds her own fate far worse. Not only has Cassandra sustained great personal losses, but she is about to die as a slave. By contrast, the nightingale not only lives, but also flies free.

[32] "Oh, Scamander" (p. 127).

The Scamander was one of the two major rivers of Troy. The other was the Simois (see note 20).

[33] "on the banks of Cocytus and sad Acheron" (p. 127).

The Cocytus and the Acheron are the two major rivers of the underworld. Cassandra is saying that she is about to die.

[34] "A brother loved his brother's wife" (p. 130).

Thyestes loved his brother Atreus' wife (see "Thyestes' Feast," pp. 21–22). Compare the king and queen in Shakespeare's *Hamlet*.

[35] "The two of us will die, but not unavenged! (p. 137).

Cassandra is predicting that she and Agamemnon will be killed but that they will be avenged (see note 38).

[36] "Orestes shall return home . . . and make an end to the evil upon evil within his family" (p. 137).

A literal translation of the Greek is as follows: The son shall return "and place a coping stone on the evils within his family." A coping stone (not to be confused with a keystone) is one of a string of crown stones on top of a stone wall or other stonework. A coping stone finishes a piece of stonework.

This startling and strange metaphor means that Orestes is going to avenge his father's death by killing his mother. The coping stone image tells us even more. As a coping stone completes a stone wall, Clytemnestra's death will somehow bring the curse on the House of Atreus to completion. This is our first clue that the blood for blood theme portrayed in *AGAMEMNON* is going to come to an end.

37 "I am not a bird shrieking in vain over horrors done in a bush!" (p. 140).

Cassandra is saying that she is not a mother bird who is distraught and shrieking because a snake or cat has gotten the baby birds. She dismisses such commonplace events among animals as trivial in comparison to human suffering and irrelevant in the lives of human beings. By her dismissal of this kind of event, Aeschylus once more shows his disdain for bird omens. Cassandra is talking about an authentic mortal concern — murder.

38 "when a woman is killed in payment for me, and a man is killed in payment for that miserably mated man" (p. 140).

Cassandra is predicting that Clytemnestra will be killed in payment for Cassandra's death and that Aegisthus will be killed in payment for Agamemnon's death. This expands upon her previous statement (see note 35).

To learn whether Cassandra's prophecy comes true, we must consult the second play of the *Orestea*. In that play, Orestes does murder Clytemnestra and Aegisthus — but not to avenge Cassandra's death. Orestes kills Clytemnestra in payment for her murder of Agamemnon, and Orestes kills Aegisthus in payment for his adultery with Clytemnestra. No one pays for Cassandra's murder. In fact, Cassandra's name is not even mentioned in the second play of the *Orestea*, nor in the third.

Is Cassandra losing her prophetic skills? No, not where *AGAMEMNON* is concerned. The trilogy must not be viewed as one grand play in which each individual play is one act. Rather, each play must be seen as complete in itself. Each play has integrity and consistency within itself. However, apart from the theme of mankind giving up vengeance and exchanging it for justice, there is a lack of consistency between the plays of the trilogy as a whole. This did not trouble Aeschylus or the theatergoers of ancient Greece because they viewed each play of a trilogy as a complete entity in itself, related to the other plays only in theme or family.

In the second play of the *Orestea*, the central conflict is Orestes' need to avenge his father's death even though it means killing his mother. To make this conflict clear and the play dramatically satisfying, Aeschylus portrays Clytemnestra as entirely deserving of death and Agamemnon as entirely flawless or perfect, and therefore undeserving of death. To make Agamemnon perfect, Aeschylus has to ignore Cassandra, whom Agamemnon brought home as his mistress in *AGAMEMNON*. Moreover, if, in the second play, Orestes were to argue that he must murder Clytemnestra because she killed both Agamemnon and Cassandra, that argument would make his case too strong and thereby reduce the conflict and tension in the play. Finally, Orestes' major ally in matricide is the god Apollo, who would never help Orestes avenge Cassandra because Apollo himself is instrumental in Cassandra's death in *AGAMEMNON*. Cassandra says Apollo "has destroyed me" (p. 122) and "Apollo is through with me, his oracle. That's why he's led me to this house of death" (p. 137).

To complete his portrayal of Agamemnon as perfect in the second play, Aeschylus also has to ignore Iphigenia, the daughter whom Agamemnon sacrificed. Therefore, in the second play — and the third play, too — Iphigenia, like Cassandra, is never mentioned. Even Clytemnestra does not mention Agamemnon's murder of Iphigenia. Never mentioned, either, is Agamemnon's ruthless annihilation of Troy — nor his army's massacre of the Trojan men, desecration of the Trojan temples, and rape and enslavement of the Trojan women.

This marked variation among the three plays shows that Aeschylus did not consider the trilogy a single grand play in three acts.

[39] "Let every man suggest a plan" (p. 143).

Aeschylus chooses the most suspenseful moment of the play to create a satire on Athenian democracy's ineffectiveness during a crisis. To give a lesson in civics — and to do so in comedy — at the moment of Agamemnon's death is another example not only of Aeschylus' startling contrasts but also of his genius.

[40] "Look at him! The lady-killer!" (p. 151).

The Greek here literally means *woman-destroyer*, but in the context of the scene and Clytemnestra's speech, it also has the meaning of the English idiom *lady-killer*, a man who is extremely attractive to women. Therefore, I conclude that the ancient Greeks had the same idiom, and I have translated it so. *Lady-killer* is especially appropriate because it not only conveys the double entendre of its literal and figurative meanings, but also it is sarcastic for both meanings. And Clytemnestra is conveying all these ideas in this speech.

Literally, Agamemnon is a *woman-destroyer*. He destroyed Iphigenia, his daughter, by murdering her. Clytemnestra has referred to that murder immediately preceding this speech. Agamemnon also destroyed Clytemnestra in the sense that as the mother of the murdered Iphigenia, Clytemnestra was devastated — *destroyed* — by Agamemnon's act. He also destroyed Cassandra, lying dead at his side, by bringing her home as his mistress.

Figuratively, Agamemnon is a *lady-killer* not only because he took Cassandra as his mistress, but also because it was he, according to Clytemnestra in the very next line, "who satisfied all the young virgins of Troy!" (p. 151). However, Clytemnestra has no evidence to support this remark.

In short, Clytemnestra is making a mockery of Agamemnon's life *and* death. She is saying, in effect, "Look at him! The *lady-killer* has been killed by a lady!"

[41] "Faithful mistress — and yet, against her breast she knew the feel of a sailor's chest" (p. 152).

Clytemnestra is casting aspersions on her husband's mistress by implying that although Agamemnon considered Cassandra "faithful," she was so flagrantly promiscuous that she had sex with anyone, including the sailors on the ship carrying them to Greece. As in note 40, Clytemnestra has no evidence for this.

In the Greek text, Clytemnestra literally says that although Cassandra was Agamemnon's "faithful mistress," she was "equally familiar with the sailors' benches." To an ancient audience, this would conjure up an image of Cassandra leaving the king's berth and going to the rowing benches of the sailors to engage in sexual acts with them. I selected the image of a sailor's chest as a more effective image for a modern audience than sailors' benches.

[42] "descendants of Tantalus!" (p. 153).

Tantalus was the grandfather of Atreus and Thyestes, the great-grandfather of Agamemnon, Menelaus, and Aegisthus, and the great-great-grandfather of Orestes.

[43] "like-minded women" (p. 154).

Helen and Clytemnestra, half-sisters, are "like-minded." Both are strong-willed, self-centered, and hubristic.

[44] "has gorged himself three times" (p. 154).

The "three times" are the murders of Thyestes' children, of Iphigenia, and of Agamemnon.

[45] "How can you say *I* did this? There is no way you can say this was done by Agamemnon's queen. Vengeance did this!" (p. 155).

Clytemnestra is suddenly absolving herself of all responsibility in Agamemnon's death. She had nothing to do with it, she says. It was all done by that Demon Vengeance who lives in the House of Atreus.

She is suddenly taking advantage of that philosophical puzzle, so beloved by the ancient Greek playwrights and philosophers (and modern philosophers, too), determinism vs. free will.

Aeschylus, until now, has led us to believe that he believes in free will (and that Clytemnestra does, too) — that people choose to do good or evil and must take responsibility for their choice. On the other hand, Aeschylus — and his character Clytemnestra — are aware of the concept of determinism (with concomitant absolution from personal responsibility), and they take full advantage of this moment to embrace it.

It is the perfect moment. Shortly before this speech, the chorus leader says, "O the Demon that crushes this House containing descendants of Tantalus!" (p. 153). Clytemnestra quickly agrees: "Ah! Now you've invoked the right spirit — Demon Vengeance, who lives in this family" (p. 154). The prophet further strengthens her case — so strongly, in fact, that Clytemnestra cannot be held accountable: "Zeus . . . causes everything . . . brings about everything. What can happen without God? What comes to fulfillment without Him?" (p. 154).

In short, Aeschylus here places before the audience that preeminent philosophical puzzle: How much of what we do comes about through determinism (for which we ought to bear no responsibility) and how much of what we do comes about through free will (for which we ought to bear full responsibility)? Clytemnestra suddenly claims no responsibility for Agamemnon's death — and she gets away with it, at least in *AGAMEMNON*. But she doesn't get away with it in the subsequent two plays of the *Orestea*. (See note 38.)

46 "From the father" (p. 156).
   Atreus is the "father."

⁴⁷ "the right instrument" (p. 156).

The chorus is talking to Clytemnestra, who killed Agamemnon and who has just been called "that Demon's tool" (p. 156). However, the chorus clearly has in mind not only Clytemnestra but also Aegisthus. Aegisthus is the nephew of Atreus and the cousin of Agamemnon — and therefore is "kindred blood" (p. 156). Aegisthus conspired with Clytemnestra. Therefore, Clytemnestra and Aegisthus together were "the right instrument."

⁴⁸ "SOLDIERS *carry* CASSANDRA'*s corpse behind the scenes. They then lift* AGAMEMNON'*s corpse . . . and carry it . . . downstage*" (p. 157).

These stage directions are consistent with the text because when Aegisthus — who notices everything — enters, he makes no note of Cassandra. He is not expecting a second murder, nor does he mention one. Moreover, moving Agamemnon's corpse downstage brings the action to where it is most effective.

⁴⁹ "For once you've predicted the future!" (p. 159).

Clytemnestra's pointed sarcasm is directed at Calchas the prophet. He has just delivered the Victor Today — Vanquished Tomorrow speech (p. 159), which reiterates a recurring theme of the play: vengeance for vengeance, blood for blood. The prophet points out the dilemma that blood-for-blood vengeance presents to mortals: On the one hand, "this truth stands eternal at the throne of God: 'Whoever does evil must pay'"; on the other hand, when human beings employ vengeance for vengeance, "Justice is impossible to attain" because the chain of blood for blood can never be broken, and such "justice" will end up destroying humanity. Clytemnestra, hitherto unimpressed with Calchas, agrees with this pessimistic prophecy.

How to punish evil and achieve justice without causing an endless chain of vengeance for vengeance is the problem presented in *AGAMEMNON* and also in the second play of the *Orestea*, in which Orestes kills his own mother, Clytemnestra, in revenge for his father, Agamemnon. The problem is ostensibly solved in the third play, when Athena, the Goddess of Wisdom, takes vengeance out of the hands of the victim's family and establishes the court of law to dispense justice dispassionately. It may come as a surprise to some that this solution was not new with Aeschylus. The court on Mars Hill in Athens existed long before Aeschylus wrote the *Orestea*.

AGAMEMNON asks a much deeper question than how a civilized society can achieve justice in the case of the murder of an individual. *AGAMEMNON* asks how mankind and the gods can achieve justice in the case of the murder of a multitude — a nation — Troy: "the anger of the massacred may never go to sleep" (p. 65) and "The gods mark those that massacre" (p. 72). The issue of the death of a nation — and how justice is achieved for such an enormous and horrendous crime — is never again addressed in the *Orestea*. That is understandable. No one has answered the question of achieving justice in the case of genocide even in our own time. That Aeschylus asked such a great question, however, shows what a great mind he had. That he asks it only in *AGAMEMNON* is but one of the many reasons that, in my judgment, the most important play in the trilogy is *AGAMEMNON*.

SELECTED SOURCES

Aeschylus. *Agamemnon* [Greek text]. In *Aeschylus II*, translated by Herbert Weir Smyth. Loeb Classical Library. Cambridge, MA: Harvard University Press; London: Wm. Heinemann Ltd., [1926] 1957.

Aristotle. *Poetics*. In *Aristotle XXIII*, edited and translated by Stephen Halliwell. Loeb Classical Library. Cambridge, MA, and London: Harvard University Press, 1995.

Denniston, J. D., and D. L. Page, eds. *Aeschylus Agamemnon.* Oxford: Clarendon Press, Oxford University Press, 1957.

Easterling, P. E., ed. *The Cambridge Companion to Greek Tragedy.* Cambridge: Cambridge University Press, 1997.

Easterling, P. E., and B. M. W. Knox, eds. *The Cambridge History of Classical Literature.* Vol. 1: *Greek Literature*, Part 2 *Greek Drama.* Cambridge: Cambridge University Press, [1989] 1995.

Garvie, A. F. *Aeschylus' Supplices: Play and Trilogy.* Cambridge: Cambridge University Press, 1969.

Hamilton, Edith. *The Greek Way.* New York: W. W. Norton & Company, Inc., [1930] 1943.

Hamilton, Edith. *Mythology*. Boston: Little, Brown & Company, 1942.

Hamilton, Edith, trans. *Three Greek Plays: Prometheus Bound, Agamemnon, The Trojan Women.* New York: W. W. Norton & Company, Inc., Norton Library, [1937] 1958.

Homer. *The Iliad.* Vol. 1. Translated by A. T. Murray. Loeb Classical Library. Cambridge, MA: Harvard University Press; London: Wm. Heinemann Ltd., 1924. Reprint, 1960.

Kitto, H. D. F. *Form and Meaning in Drama.* London: Methuen & Co., Ltd., University Paperbacks; New York: Barnes & Noble Inc., [1956, 1959] 1960.

Kitto, H. D. F. *The Greeks.* Harmondsworth, Middlesex, England: Penguin Books Ltd., [1951] 1962.

Lattimore, Richmond, trans. *Aeschylus I: Oresteia.* Chicago: The University of Chicago Press, 1953.

A Lexicon: Abridged from Liddell and Scott's Greek-English Lexicon. Oxford: Clarendon Press, Oxford University Press, 1958.

Liddell, Henry George, and Robert Scott. *Greek-English Lexicon.* 9th ed. Oxford: Clarendon Press, Oxford University Press, [1843] 1940.

Murray, Gilbert. *Aeschylus: The Creator of Tragedy.* London, Oxford: Clarendon Press, 1940.

Sidgwick, Arthur. "Aeschylus," *Encyclopaedia Britannica.* 11th ed. Vol. 1. New York: Encyclopaedia Britannica Company, 1910.

Smyth, Herbert Weir, trans. *Aeschylus I.* Loeb Classical Library. Cambridge, MA: Harvard University Press; London: Wm. Heinemann Ltd., [1922] 1956.

Smyth, Herbert Weir, trans. *Aeschylus II.* Loeb Classical Library. Cambridge, MA: Harvard University Press; London: Wm. Heinemann Ltd., [1926] 1957. [Contains the Greek text of *AGAMEMNON.*]

Tussman, Joseph. *The Burden of Office: Agamemnon and Other Losers.* Vancouver, BC, Canada: Talonbooks, 1989.